"Terry Polakovic has long been one of our [leading?] [voices on the?] nature and dignity of women. In her new [book?], [she offers?] an insightful reading of more than a century of papal teachings on marriage and family. As we approach the fiftieth anniversary of Pope Paul VI's *Humanae Vitae*, Polakovic provides a timely reminder that the Church's teachings are not about rules and regulations, but about opening our hearts to God and trusting his beautiful plan for our lives."

— *Archbishop José H. Gomez, archbishop of Los Angeles*

"Terry Polakovic's work on behalf of the dignity of women, deeply rooted in her Catholic faith, has been extraordinary for many years. In *Life and Love*, she gives us an insightful, beautifully written guide to the Christian meaning of sexuality, marriage, family, and love grounded in a century of Church teaching. It's a joy to read, and essential for anyone eager for an engaging introduction to Catholic thought on these vital matters."

— *Archbishop Charles J. Chaput, O.F.M.Cap., archbishop of Philadelphia*

"As our married and family life emerges within the plan of God, we know and experience the blessings and fruitfulness of God. In *Life and Love*, Terry Polakovic re-proposes the most important wisdom on marriage and the family in modern times. If you desire to know the blessings and fruitfulness of God in your marriage and family, you would do well to engage with this important work."

— *Dan Burke, executive director of the National Catholic Register and president of the Avila Institute for Spiritual Formation*

"This excellent little book unfolds the Church's teachings on life and love in a fresh, creative way. Author Terry Polakovic sets *Humanae Vitae* within a rich historical context: she links it to seven other pivotal Church documents, offering fascinating details about the popes who wrote them and the societal challenges they addressed. A delightful read, it includes questions for personal reflection or group discussion at the end of each chapter. Highly recommended!"

— *Mary Rice Hasson, director, Catholic Women's Forum, and Kate O'Beirne Fellow, Catholic Studies Program, Ethics and Public Policy Center*

"*Life and Love* so beautifully roots *Humanae Vitae* in the Church's rich historical tradition, reminding us that the Church has never abandoned us but has reoriented and guided the world throughout the centuries. It points us to this fact today: that we, too, must reorient our hearts to receive truth and carry that truth of Christ to the culture in new ways."

— *Katherine Meeks, executive director of Endow*
(Educating on the Nature and Dignity of Women)

"Terry Polakovic has done the Church a great service by writing a book that invites us to delve deeper into the truth and beauty of human sexuality through the teaching documents of the Church. This book is an excellent resource for individuals, parish groups, married couples, and families. It deserves a place in every Catholic home."

— *Steve Weidenkopf, lecturer in Church History*
at the Christendom College Graduate School

"Never fear a papal encyclical again. After you read this book, you will possess a genuine understanding and even a personal affection for the popes, the teachings, and the courage that comprise centuries of Catholic teaching about sex, marriage, and parenting. Never dry, complicated, cold, or antiquated, this historical tour is current, essential, and intrinsically interesting, especially in light of the dramatic questions that confront us today."

— *Helen Alvaré, professor of law, Scalia Law School at George Mason University*

Life and Love

LIFE AND LOVE

OPENING YOUR HEART
TO GOD'S DESIGN

TERRY POLAKOVIC

Our Sunday Visitor
www.osv.com
Our Sunday Visitor Publishing
Our Sunday Visitor, Inc
Huntington, Indiana 46750

Nihil Obstat:
Msgr. Michael Heintz, Ph.D.
Censor Librorum

Imprimatur:
✠ Kevin C. Rhoades
Bishop of Fort Wayne-South Bend
May 7, 2018

The *Nihil Obstat* and *Imprimatur* are official declarations that a book is free from doctrinal or moral error. It is not implied that those who have granted the *Nihil Obstat* and *Imprimatur* agree with the contents, opinions, or statements expressed.

ABOUT THE AUTHOR

Terry Polakovic lives in Denver, Colorado, with her husband, Mike. They have two adult children. Terry is one of the cofounders of Endow (Educating on the Nature and Dignity of Women) and served as president of the organization from 2003 to 2015. She worked in nonprofit leadership for more than 30 years and is now retired. In 2010, she received the Pro Ecclesia et Pontifice Cross award ("For the Church and Pontiff") from Pope Benedict XVI. In 2011, Terry was recognized as an "Outstanding Catholic Leader" by the Catholic Leadership Institute.

To my husband, Mike,
with much love and appreciation

CONTENTS

INTRODUCTION

It has been fifty years since the promulgation of Pope Paul VI's encyclical *Humanae Vitae* ("Of Human Life"), and the fact that we still count the years speaks volumes. Since its release in 1968, there has been no doubt that the truth *Humanae Vitae* (on the regulation of birth) affirms can be a tough sell. Still today, there are those who do not understand the document, who try to manipulate the content, and who refuse to see it for what it is: Church teaching that does not stand alone and must be placed in the context of "everything important and fruitful the Church has said on marriage and family during these last fifty years."[1]

Despite the Church's constant teaching that the use of contraception is intrinsically wrong, in today's culture using contraception is seen as a good, as the morally and socially right and responsible thing to do. This misunderstanding persists even among many well-meaning Catholics. In fact, I remember a time several years ago when I was teaching high school girls about this very encyclical. They got it. Every girl in that room declared that she wanted to have the kind of marriage Pope Paul VI described: one in which both spouses offer each other faithful, free, total, and self-giving love. And to have such a marriage, these girls were willing to save sexual intimacy until they married.

What happened next, I could never have anticipated. Two of the mothers called to tell me that what I was teaching their daughters conflicted with what they were teaching at home! They were naturally upset, but what I found more disturbing was that no one had ever taught these Catholic mothers about the teachings found

11

in *Humanae Vitae* or even encouraged them to read it. What I had shared with their daughters was completely foreign to them.

Today, far too many Catholics have never read or learned about *Humanae Vitae*. And among those who do know the document, far too many believe it is only about contraception. Yet reading it with an open mind reveals that it is about so much more. Opening your heart to the wisdom of *Humanae Vitae* is life-transforming. I have both experienced it and witnessed it. Although it is best known as the document regarding the Church's teaching on contraception, it is really about much more — it is about letting go and trusting God. It's about embracing all human life — and living it — as God intended. If we can give the most intimate part of ourselves, our sexuality, to God, then we can surely trust him with everything else. Moreover, if we do this month after month, it becomes a habit, and before long we have developed the habit of trusting God with the parts of our lives that really matter. What a gift!

Today, we are living in a time and in a culture that Pope Saint John Paul II coined a "culture of death," and we have been living in it for a long time, more than a hundred years. Someone once told me that the culture of death means that someone has to die to solve a problem. To be sure, we just need to look around to see that there is death everywhere. Violence, war, capital punishment, abortion, euthanasia, suicide, you name it. It is everywhere. At first glance, it may not be apparent that the culture of death and all that it entails is related to the use of contraception. However, the connection is present. Contraception introduced the idea that life is disposable, that we, in fact, have the power to reject it. Violence, war, capital punishment, etc., are all, at root, manifestations of rejecting life.

Sadly, we are all a product of this culture of death in one way or another. According to John Paul II, it is culture, not politics or economics, that drives history. His biographer George Weigel explains St. John Paul's thought: "Culture was, is, and always will be the most dynamic force in history, allowing us to resist tyranny and inspiring us to build and sustain free societies. Moreover, [John Paul II] understood that at the center of culture is cult, or religion: what people believe, cherish, and worship; what people are willing to stake their lives, and their children's lives, on."[2]

It is not surprising, then, that John Paul II strongly believed that the Church is in the position to shape the culture by helping to change the way people think and act. In order to effect the kind of change that John Paul envisioned, however, we must be able to see what the Church sees, to think with the "mind of the Church." This means, "When we look out upon the universe, we see the same universe that the Church sees."[3] We normally look at things in the moment, in relationship to ourselves. In contrast, the Church always sees things in totality, in relationship to the whole according to the plan of God.

The culture of death might be painfully apparent and pervasive, but we can have hope. Life is also pervasive, and it is much more powerful than death. This is the life-giving joy we find in Christ and his Church. In every day and age, the Church proposes the antidote to the culture of selfishness and destruction. In his book *The Splendor of The Church*, Henri de Lubac tells us: "The Church is in the world, and by the effect of her presence alone she communicates to it an unrest that cannot be soothed away. She is a perpetual witness to the Christ who came 'to shake human life to its foundations.'"[4] This is exactly why *Humanae Vitae* often makes people uncomfortable. The truth can set you free, but it can also make you squirm.

We live in a fallen world, and as such we need help seeing the universe as God sees it — this is where the teaching role of the Church comes in. For this reason, the Church issues teaching documents, such as *Humanae Vitae*. Given that this book is being written specifically to highlight the fiftieth anniversary of *Humanae Vitae*, it is helpful to place that encyclical in its proper context, particularly as it relates to other Church teachings. Pope

Paul VI did not write *Humanae Vitae* out of the blue. No, as a matter of fact, there were many things happening in the world that led to that monumental document, and many more monumental things have happened since that show us the continued urgency of the Church's teaching on human life and human love.

Popes do not choose encyclical topics randomly or by chance. Rather, encyclicals are written as an encouragement, as an explanation, and many times as a warning in response to the signs of the times. More importantly, these documents are part of the Church's participation in humanity's ongoing dialogue. Over the course of this book, we will take a deeper look not only at *Humanae Vitae*,[5] but at seven other teaching documents — not all encyclicals — on the themes of life and love, two that precede *Humanae Vitae* and five that follow it.

In doing so, we will survey 140 years of official Catholic teaching pertaining to authentic love, life, marriage, and family. In a sense, this book is a "slice of life" regarding these important subjects seen over the span of more than a century. By drawing from these documents, we will see exactly how the Church, an "'expert in humanity,' places herself at the service of every individual and of the whole world."[6]

To begin, we will look at the encyclical *Arcanum* (on Christian marriage), written by Pope Leo XIII in 1880, during the Industrial Revolution. Although many good things came from the Industrial Revolution, it also produced significant changes in society, particularly concerning the family. The change from an agrarian to an industrial society led to the rise of urban areas where people (both men and women) left the home to "go to work." This was a significant cultural shift, which had an effect on marriages as never before.

During this time, the first legal steps to loosening divorce laws were made. When Pope Leo XIII wrote *Arcanum* early in his pontificate, he was seriously worried about the state of marriage in the nineteenth century. Leo used this document to reaffirm the meaning of sacramental marriage in a world that was rapidly changing, a world that seemed to disregard the grave impact these changes were having upon the family, the basic cell of society.

From there we will look at the 1930 encyclical *Casti Connubii* ("Of Chaste Marriage"), written by Pope Pius XI. World War I, the "war to end all wars," was more than a decade previous, but the world was now in the throes of the Great Depression. Margaret Sanger's American Birth Control League was gaining popularity, and the birth control mentality was seeping into marriages because the severely weakened economy made people feel desperate. In *Casti Connubii*, Pius XI defended marriage as a divine institution, placing a special emphasis on birth control, which he claimed was the principal threat against the sanctity of marriage in modern times.

Humanae Vitae was promulgated right at the height of the sexual revolution. The birth control pill, released in 1960, inflamed and made possible this revolution of "free love" — a revolution that continues unabated in the present day. Prior to 1930, all Christian churches taught that contraception was intrinsically evil. However, by the 1960s, the only church officially and visibly teaching against contraception was the Catholic Church. Many Catholics were hoping that the Church would follow the other Christian denominations and change her teachings on this controversial subject.

In response to this climate of confusion, and after years of prayer, consultation, commissions, and study, Pope Paul VI issued *Humanae Vitae* on July 25, 1968. To the surprise of many, the document affirmed the Church's consistent teaching against contraception — a teaching dating back to the early Church. It turned out to be a prophetic document, listing social ills that were sure to occur (many of which have since occurred) with the normalization of contraception.

Next, we will explore *Familiaris Consortio* (on the role of the Christian family in the modern world), written by Pope John Paul

II in 1981. It addresses all of the elements of the family that have come under fire in the current culture, reminding us of the true, the good, and the beautiful of the profound gift of family. By the early 1980s, many of Pope Paul VI's predictions had come true. The divorce rate had hit an all-time high, with nearly 50 percent of first marriages ending in divorce.[7] In this document, John Paul II zeroed in on the relationship between husband and wife, especially as it pertains to their openness to children and the responsibilities of parenthood. He stressed that the Church has a profound interest in everything that pertains to the family, reminding us, "The future of humanity passes by way of the family."[8]

In 1988, John Paul II released his beautiful meditation *Mulieris Dignitatem* (on the dignity and vocation of women) in response to the ever-increasing, ever-dangerous, secular feminist movement. This feminist ideology promoted the belief that there is no difference between men and women, that we are not only equal, but equivalent in all respects. Today the culture has taken it one step further, believing that a person can be a man or a woman or fifty other things, or even nothing at all.

Mulieris Dignitatem brings us back to the truth about men and women, indeed equal in dignity, but not the same. In this meditation, in an effort to see what God intended for the human race, John Paul II looked back to the beginning, to the creation of man and woman in the Book of Genesis. He spoke to the gift of womanhood, encouraging all women to follow in the footsteps of our Blessed Mother. The meditation ends with a plea to the women of the world, challenging them to use their "feminine genius" to create a culture of life.

Nearly ten years later, in 1995, John Paul II continued his great teaching pontificate with *Evangelium Vitae* ("The Gospel of Life"). Here, for the first time in his pontificate, John Paul introduced the concepts of "a culture of life" and "a culture of death." He addressed the countless ways in which human life is threatened in the present day and reiterated the Church's view on its inestimable value, warning against the dangers of violating the sanctity of life. The primary focus of this groundbreaking encyclical was on the human right to life, taking a hard look at hot-button issues, including abortion, birth control, and euthanasia. The late pope also explored other concepts relevant to embryology, such as in vitro fertilization, sterilization, embryonic-stem-cell research, and fetal experimentation. He also addressed the death penalty.

On Christmas Day 2005, Pope Benedict XVI published the first encyclical of his pontificate, *Deus Caritas Est* ("God Is Love"). Convinced that the world had lost the true meaning of love, Pope Benedict used this encyclical to reaffirm what love means to us as human beings, especially in a culture that seeks to redefine it as anything that fulfills the individual. First, he compared the great gift of *eros* (romantic love) with the love that God reveals in Jesus Christ, showing how the human desire for *eros* is confirmed, elevated, and transformed in the love of God. Next, he offered a meditation on how love is to be "organized" in society, concluding that ideological motivations for reordering society are different from the motivation provided by Jesus Christ. If "charitable activity is to maintain all of its splendor and not become just another form of social assistance,"[9] it must be centered on Christ and performed for God's glory alone.

The last document is *Amoris Laetitia* ("The Joy of Love"), written by Pope Francis in 2016. When asked in the summer of 2017 if the Church was going to take up the theme of birth control once again, Pope Francis (who has shown strong support of both Pope Paul VI and his encyclical) responded, "All of this depends on how 'Humanae Vitae' is interpreted."[10] He added, "The question is not that of changing the doctrine but of going deeper and making pastoral (ministry) take into account the situations and that which it is possible for people to do."[11] Francis wants the Church to reach out with mercy to those who have found the Church's teachings difficult or who have reaped the negative consequences of the vast cultural changes affecting so many lives.

In the following chapters we will take a close look at these eight Church documents that pertain to human life — its dignity, its mystery, and its complexity. In addition to *Humanae Vitae*, I have chosen to focus on the other seven documents for two reasons. First, they provide both historical and theological context for the central precepts of *Humanae Vitae*. And, quite simply, they articulate the Church's teachings that are most significant for the survival of a civilization in which the human person is fully valued, empowered, and able to flourish in accordance with the plan of God.

CHAPTER ONE

The Times, They Are a-Changing

Leo XIII, *Arcanum Divinae*

MAN, MACHINE, AND THE MANIFESTO

On the morning of Monday, October 13, 1884, Pope Leo XIII had a vision that would surely haunt him for the rest of his days. He had just finished celebrating Mass in one of the Vatican's private chapels for a few cardinals and members of his household staff. After the Mass, he stopped at the foot of the altar and stayed there for about ten minutes, as if in a trance, his face ashen white. Then, suddenly, he collapsed from what appeared to be a heart attack or a stroke. Shortly thereafter, however, he arose, immediately went to his office, and composed the prayer to Saint Michael. Later, the pope gave instructions to all the faithful to recite this prayer after all low Masses. God had shown him the future of the Church that he loved so much, and there was more than enough reason to be alarmed.[12]

Pope Leo later explained that he had heard two voices — one kind and gentle, the other guttural and harsh. He recalled the prideful voice of Satan boasting to Our Lord:

> "I can destroy your Church." To which the gentle
> voice of Our Lord replied, "You can? Then go ahead
> and do so." Satan answered, "To do so, I need more
> time and more power." The Lord said, "How much
> time? How much power?" "75 to 100 years, and a
> greater power over those who will give themselves
> over to my service," was Satan's reply. Mysteriously
> our Lord said, "You have the time, you have the
> power. Do with them what you will."[13]

Today, we know that this short exchange prophesied a time of darkness and evil. The twentieth century would see much darkness, in the form of wars, immorality, genocide, and all out apostasy. It would be a century of martyrs.

Prior to the pontificate of Pope Leo XIII, the Catholic Church of the nineteenth century had been under siege and on the defensive. However, under Leo XIII, the Church would rally and boldly respond to the challenges of the day, gaining the moral high ground "where she had [previously] lost physical territory and political support."[14] During his nearly twenty-six years in office, he wrote a record eighty-five encyclicals. *Arcanum* (on Christian marriage) was the fourth.

Gioacchino Pecci, the future Pope Leo XIII, was born in 1810, in the midst of the nineteenth-century Industrial Revolution. His was an era of extremes. From the moment of his birth, it was clear that the world was already changing in monumental ways. Never before had the lives of so many men and women changed more dramatically in the course of only a century.

The invention of railroads, telephones, the telegraph, electricity, mass production, forged steel, automobiles, and countless other modern discoveries transformed the world at a dizzying pace and well beyond anyone's wildest dreams. What began in Great

Britain quickly spread to North America, Japan, and Western Europe, as well as other parts of the world. As Walter Carroll writes in his book *The Crisis of Christendom*, "The Industrial Revolution transformed the world forever ... it led to the Age of Enterprise, which created wealth and raised the standard of living to a degree unheard of in human history."[15]

However, change did not come easy. For better and for worse, the Industrial Revolution had a profound impact on the family. It altered traditional values, roles, and behaviors, influencing all aspects of life and culture:

> The Industrial Revolution, with its influx of workers from the farms into the cities to find work in the factories, raised new economic problems, and made possible a new sort of poverty. The worker, who on the farm would never have been absolutely without, was now dependent entirely upon the wages he earned. He had at his disposal no land to cultivate, no livestock; he had no investments, because he had nothing to invest. All his earthly needs had to be met from the wages he received in exchange for his labor. The poor man scratching out a living on his tiny plot of land was replaced by the poor man who had only his labor to sell. His very existence depended upon his finding work and receiving a just wage for his labor.[16]

With improved forms of transportation, people were able to move from one place to another. Consequently, laborers migrated from rural areas to towns in order to be closer to the factories in which they worked. They frequently left their families behind. The family-centered focus of economic life changed to a focus on each separate individual. The hours were long and the work was grueling; for many, working conditions were deplorable. Not surprisingly, marriages suffered, birth rates declined, and year after year divorce rates increased. These harsh and seemingly hopeless realities led to a decrease in faith, which resulted in a decrease in church attendance.

As all this was happening, an unknown political theorist named Karl Marx was living in exile[17] in Brussels writing one of history's most influential texts. In 1848, together with his financier and fellow author, Friedrich Engels, Marx released his ideas in the form of a pamphlet called *The Communist Manifesto*.[18] With this small booklet, the father of communism set in motion a tidal wave of social change. His ideology would have far-reaching consequences, affecting the lives of millions of people around the world throughout the nineteenth and twentieth centuries, and still today.

The Communist Manifesto was written to propose solutions to the problems created by industrialization. Based on the idea that the "history of all hitherto existing societies is the history of class struggles,"[19] the *Manifesto* provided a narrative for how the "capitalist society of the time would eventually be replaced by Socialism, and then eventually Communism."[20]

Marx intended to provide a foundation for practical answers to the miseries of the working class that had been created by the Industrial Revolution. His solution to these problems was to establish a society in which the state owns and operates everything and gives to all its citizens according to their predetermined need. In a society such as this, competition in economic endeavors simply does not exist. There is no private property, no free market, and, most especially, no God.

Leo XIII used strong words to describe the negative consequences of these beliefs. He even went so far as to call Marx's socialist ideas a "deadly plague that is creeping into the very fibers of human society and leading it on to the verge of destruction."[21] Pope Leo warned that this kind of socialism seeks to destroy the institution of marriage and the sacredness of the family. He asserted that the "foundation of this society rests first of all in the indissoluble union of man and wife according to the necessity of natural law."[22] Yet, the "doctrines of Socialism strive almost completely to dissolve this union."[23]

In Karl Marx's very design, the state usurps the rights and functions of the family, "shattering society into tiny atoms whirling around a single nucleus: the federal government."[24] While socialists such as Marx thought in only two categories — the individual and the state — our Catholic faith teaches us that "society and the state exist for the family."[25] *Arcanum Divinae* was the first document of its kind, in that it "single-handedly inaugurated modern Catholic teaching on marriage and family."[26]

ARCANUM DIVINAE

Blessed John Henry Newman once paid Pope Leo XIII the ultimate compliment by saying that he had the "virtue of humanity."[27] For a century, Pope Leo guided human hearts, soothed their pain and sorrow, all while pointing "his finger upward to the higher places of the better life."[28] He was known for his firmness, his gentleness, his frugality, and his broad generosity, all at the same time. Indeed, these are the characteristics that stand out in his encyclical letter that focused on Christian marriage. As he crafted it, he was well aware of the suffering and desperation that had overcome so many people, particularly those in the working class. When they bled, he bled. Nevertheless, he was convinced that the truth really does set us free.

In writing this document, Pope Leo's main concern was the secularization of marriage. He attributed this to: (1) the separation of the secular marriage contract from the Catholic Church's Sacrament of Matrimony; (2) the rise in the number of lawful divorces; and (3) a society that was becoming totally degraded by its abandonment of God.[29] Pope Leo laid all of these negative consequences at the feet of socialism (the "state"), which he had renounced in another document two years earlier. He positively rejected Marx and his socialist ideas because of their adverse effects on the family. He argued that the family has priority over the state; that, in fact, there would be no state without the family.

Leo used *Arcanum* to clarify the lines between the Church and the state, particularly related to marriage and family. "Since family life is the germ of society, and marriage is the basis of family life, the healthy condition of civil no less than of religious society depends on the inviolability of the marriage contract."[30]

Pope Leo was "ever at pains to show that the Church does for the state what the state cannot well do for itself: she makes citizens of the city of God, citizens who make for something like a just city here below."[31] He warned against those who would remove marriage from the sovereignty of God by withdrawing it from the jurisdiction of the Church and turning it into a simple civil contract. This, he taught, strips marriage of its sacredness and reduces it to a "common secular thing."[32] He wrote repeatedly that marriage is part of God's natural law, and as such the state cannot claim what rightly belongs to God.

"What Did God Intend?"

Pope Leo introduced this encyclical on Christian marriage by placing it in its proper context, by asking the question, "What did God intend?" Since marriage is part of God's creative design for humanity, we can be sure that he had a plan, one that is very familiar to us. Looking back to the very beginning of humanity, the pope reflected:

> The true origin of marriage is ... well-known to all.... We record what is to all known, and cannot be doubted by any, that God, on the sixth day of creation, having made man from the slime of the earth, and having breathed into his face the breath of life, gave him a companion, whom He miraculously took from the side of Adam when he was locked in sleep. God thus, in His most far-reaching foresight,

decreed that this husband and wife should be the natural beginning of the human race.[33]

Even from the beginning, God's creative design for humanity came in the form of marriage between a man and a woman. This divinely inspired companionship manifests itself in "two most excellent properties — deeply sealed, as it were, and signed upon it — namely, *unity* and *perpetuity*."[34] In other words, God intended marriage to be exclusive and until the death of one spouse.

Yet the pope well understood that in a fallen world hearts are easily hardened. He recognized all too well that, through human weakness and willfulness, marriage became corrupted; Scripture and ancient history reveal all too plainly how polygamy destroyed marriage's unity, and divorce its perpetuity:[35]

> This form of marriage, however, so excellent and so preeminent, began to be corrupted by degrees, and to disappear among the heathen; and became even among the Jewish race clouded in a measure and obscured. For in their midst a common custom was gradually introduced, by which it was accounted as lawful for a man to have more than one wife; and eventually when "by reason of the hardness of their heart" [Mt 19:8], Moses indulgently permitted them to put away their wives, [and then] the way was open to divorce.[36]

We as Christians thus have so much to be thankful for, because through the mercy of God and in the fullness of time our Savior, Jesus Christ, came to restore "the world, which was sinking, as it were, with length of years into decline."[37] Indeed, Christ came to make "all things new" (Rv 21:5):

> Christ our Lord, setting himself to fulfill the com-

mandment, which His Father had given Him, straightway imparted a new form and fresh beauty to all things, taking away the effects of their time-worn age. For He healed the wounds which the sin of our first father had inflicted on the human race; He brought all men, by nature children of wrath, into favor with God; He led to the light of truth men wearied out by long-standing errors; He renewed to every virtue those who were weakened by lawlessness of every kind; and, giving them again an inheritance of never ending bliss, He added a sure hope that their mortal and perishable bodies should one day be partakers of immortality and of the glory of heaven. In order that these unparalleled benefits might last as long as men should be found on earth, He entrusted to His Church the continuance of His work; and, looking to future times, He commanded her to set in order whatever might have become deranged in human society, and to restore whatever might have fallen into ruin.[38]

In his saving work, Christ restored the original design of human marriage and then, to sanctify more thoroughly this institution, "Christ our Lord raised the marriage contract to the dignity of a sacrament."[39] In light of this, by way of "tradition and the written word [coming] through the Apostles,"[40] the Church has always maintained that in order to uphold the dignity of marriage as a sacrament, we must think of the marriage contract and the Sacrament of Matrimony as one and the same thing. Consequently, there cannot be a marriage contract among Christians that is *not* a sacrament.

In a sacramental marriage, husband and wife are "to cherish always a very great mutual love, to be ever faithful to their marriage vow, and to give one another unfailing and unselfish help."[41] In a similar way, children are to submit to their parents and obey them, "while parents are bound to give all care and watchful thought to the education of their offspring."[42] Continuing this line of thinking, Pope Leo wrote:

> Not only ... was marriage instituted for the propagation of the human race, but also that the lives of husbands and wives might be made better and happier. This comes about in many ways: by their lightening each other's burdens through mutual help; by constant and faithful love; by having all their possessions in common; and by the heavenly grace, which flows from the sacrament.[43]

The purpose of a Christian marriage is the welfare of each of the spouses, and the ultimate goal is to bring each other to heaven. It is sacred. Beyond their focus on each other, the husband and wife must be open to new life and willing to bring "forth children for the Church, 'fellow citizens with the saints' ... so that 'a people might be born and brought up for the worship and religion of the true God and our Savior Jesus Christ.'"[44]

Because Christ raised marriage to the dignity of a sacrament, the Church has always claimed exclusive authority over it while allowing civil authorities to regulate the civil concerns and consequences of marriage. If we look at marriage through the lens of history, we see that for centuries the Church exercised that authority, and civil authorities submitted to it.

By the nineteenth century, however, human frailty and downright disobedience, as reflected in relaxed divorce laws, became more common and more acceptable. The reins of Christian restraint in family life began to loosen. This opened the door to a power grab by civil authorities, who were poised to dismiss the Church's authority over the marriage contract. These same authorities began to sow seeds of discontent by suggesting that the marriage contract was not a sacrament at all, and that the civil contract and the sacrament were two separate and distinct things.

Thus we see that the dissolubility of marriage and the relaxed view of divorce trampled upon the unity and integrity of the marriage relationship. As part of this process, the state began to restrict the rights of the Church in the area of marriage. What looked like the "separation of Church and state" was actually, in practice, the "removal of the Church from the state" and any influence she might have in the public square. In effect, the Church was gradually excluded from any civil role in decision-making, where she is both competent and wise due to her divine authority.

As the state began to exercise more power over marriage, it also assumed the right to define it, and, "ignoring its fundamental nature, it allowed such corruptions to enter into the positive laws of marriage, such as divorce and remarriage, and serial polygamy."[45] This is the mindset that led to what we now call "civil" marriages. A civil marriage is a marriage performed, recorded, and recognized by a government official. In other words, it is a marriage performed outside of the Church and without the benefit of the grace of the sacrament.

According to Pope Leo, the fundamental change from marital "indissolubility" to "dissolubility" opened the way to the sensitive topic of separation and divorce. He correctly predicted that once divorce was accepted, further moral decline would surely follow. Eventually, it would darken the conscience of society, causing — and spreading — a moral numbness:

> There will be no restraint powerful enough to keep it within the bounds marked out.... The eagerness for divorce, daily spreading by devious ways, will seize upon the minds of many like a virulent contagious disease, or like a flood of water bursting through every barrier.... So soon as the road to divorce began to be made smooth by law, at once

quarrels, jealousies, and judicial separations largely increased; and such shamelessness of life followed that men who had been in favor of these divorces repented of what they had done, and feared that, if they did not carefully seek a remedy by repealing the law, the State itself might come to ruin.[46]

Continuing to reflect on the harmfulness of divorce, Pope Leo highlighted its often-forgotten victims: the children. He also underscored the need to protect the "dignity of womanhood,"[47] which through divorce is frequently compromised. In the world of divorce, women are at risk of being used for the personal pleasures of men and then left behind to fend for themselves, frequently with a child or more in tow. Hence, from the question "What did God intend?" we must move on to ask, when we don't follow God's plan, "What are the consequences?"

What Are the Consequences?

Pope Leo wrote prophetically of the harsh consequences and raw pain for all involved when we deviate from the plan of God as it pertains to marriage. He recognized that there is no end to the painful ramifications of divorce:

> Truly, it is hardly possible to describe how great are the evils that flow from divorce. Matrimonial contracts are by it made variable; mutual kindness is weakened; deplorable inducements to unfaithfulness are supplied; harm is done to the education and training of children; occasion is afforded for the breaking up of homes; the seeds of dissension are sown among families; the dignity of womanhood is lessened and brought low, and women run the risk of being deserted after having ministered to the pleasures of men. Since,

> then, nothing has such power to lay waste families and destroy the mainstay of kingdoms as the corruption of morals, it is easily seen that divorces are in the highest degree hostile to the prosperity of families and States, springing as they do from the depraved morals of the people, and, as experience shows us, opening a way to every kind of evil-doing in public and in private life.[48]

As Pope Leo correctly predicted, one of the consequences of the disillusionment caused by the breakup of the family was cohabitation. Rather than commit to one another for a lifetime, couples choose to live together for as long as it lasts. For this reason, the pope commended to his brother bishops and priests "those unhappy persons who, carried away by the heat of passion, and being utterly indifferent to their salvation, live wickedly together without the bond of lawful marriage."[49]

As for those couples who are struggling in their marriages, and who are seriously contemplating separation? In a post-Christian world such as ours, Pope Leo's advice may seem rather simplistic. It may even offend our modern sensibilities. Even so, his counsel was to rely on faith in the Lord, the One who never disappoints, trusting in the words of Saint Paul in his Letter to the Romans: "We know that in everything God works for good [for] those who love him" (8:28). The pope wrote:

> To sum up all in a few words, there would be a calm and quiet constancy in marriage if married people would gather strength and life from the virtue of religion alone, which imparts to us resolution and fortitude; for religion would enable them to bear tranquilly and even gladly the trials of their state, such as, for instance, the faults that they discover in one another, the difference of temper and character,

the weight of a mother's cares, the wearing anxiety about the education of children, reverses of fortune, and the sorrows of life.[50]

The virtue of religion is basically giving God his due. As such it falls under the virtue of justice. The *Catechism of the Catholic Church* says: "Adoration is the first act of the virtue of religion. To adore God is to acknowledge him as God, as the Creator and Savior, the Lord and Master of everything that exists, as infinite and merciful Love."[51] Without being trite, what Leo is saying here is that instead of looking at one another, married people in difficult situations should shift their gaze to God.

Granted, there are some marriages that appear to be beyond repair. While the Church always encourages healing, forgiveness, and reconciliation, she does allow for such situations: "When, indeed, matters have come to such a pitch that it seems impossible for them to live together any longer, then the Church allows them to live apart, and strives at the same time to soften the evils of this separation by such remedies and helps as are suited to their condition; yet she never ceases to endeavor to bring about a reconciliation, and never despairs of doing so."[52]

While Pope Leo did not address them in this letter, there are some serious situations that can call into question the validity of a sacramental marriage, even if the couple was married in the Catholic Church by a priest or a deacon. In some cases, a supposed valid marriage may be, in fact, invalid for some serious reason. If a major impediment — for example, mental illness; sexual abuse; trauma; addiction to drugs, alcohol, or sex; etc. — was present at the time of the wedding, then the sacramental marriage may be invalid. In circumstances such as this, one or both spouses may start the process to obtain a declaration of nullity, commonly referred to as an annulment. An annulment is *not* a Catholic divorce. The annulment process is about determining whether a valid marriage occurred on the wedding day. If it is determined that the marriage was invalid, both parties are free to marry again, as if for the first time.

We cannot overlook the important fact that sacramental marriage is good for both the state and all of society. The Church is not the enemy; she is the best friend of the civil power and the guardian of civil society:[53]

> Marriage also can do much for the good of families, for, so long as it is conformable to nature and in accordance with the counsels of God, it has power to strengthen union of heart in the parents; to secure the holy education of children; to temper the authority of the father by the example of the divine authority; to render children obedient to their parents and servants obedient to their masters. From such marriages as these, the State may rightly expect a race of citizens animated by a good spirit and filled with reverence and love for God, recognizing it their duty to obey those who rule justly and lawfully, to love all, and to injure no one.[54]

In concluding this heartfelt letter, Pope Leo offered some additional fatherly advice. Again, his words may fly in the face of our politically correct culture, but many married couples would attest to the fact that there is wisdom here. Leo wrote:

> Care also must be taken [not] to easily enter into marriage with those who are not Catholics; for, when minds do not agree as to the observances of religion, it is scarcely possible to hope for agreement in other things. Other reasons also proving that persons should turn with dread from such marriages are chiefly these: that they give occasion to forbidden association and communion in religious mat-

ters; endanger the faith of the Catholic partner; are a hindrance to the proper education of the children; and often lead to a mixing up of truth and falsehood, and to the belief that all religions are equally good.[55]

This was not meant to be uncharitable. Rather, it came from a place of experience from one who had studied the human condition nearly all his life and took seriously his obligation to pastor the people of God. That being said, "with God all things are possible" (Mt. 19:26). This may be the perfect opportunity for the Catholic spouse to delve deeper into the Faith, and in doing so to fall ever more in love with our Lord and Savior, Jesus Christ, so that when and if the time comes, he will be prepared to defend the hope that is within him with gentleness and reverence.

Pope Leo XIII's foretelling of the pain and personal destruction that would surely come with relaxed divorce laws was truly prophetic. Today we live in a culture where divorce has become a common tragedy. In his book *Defending Marriage*, Anthony Esolen captures it all too well:

> Whole networks of human relations [have been] torn asunder; husband from wife, parents from children, aunts and uncles from their nieces and nephews ... all of that web of meaning and belonging, extending far into the past and future, untimely ripped, battered, or severed forever, to satisfy the "needs" (... nearly always selfish) of the divorcing adults.
>
> [Divorce] has touched every family in the nation. Who does not know at least one family whose children require an essay merely to describe who under their roof is related to whom and how?[56]

The tragedy of divorce is not just what it does to marriages, but what it does to all of society. If the family, the cornerstone of society, is not solid, then nothing is solid. Things that were once enduring have become transient, and all relationships are merely temporary. If a spouse cannot be trusted, everyone (and everything) is suspect.

Marriages suffer today not because modern society *listened* to the Church. Instead, marriages are suffering precisely because society *did not* listen to the Church. Now, nearly 140 years after this encyclical, we are living with the consequences of not heeding the Church's warnings about marriage.

Despite this, we are a people of hope. We believe in tomorrow, and we know that our God is a merciful God. In fact, Pope Francis never tires of speaking about the mercy of God. In his book *The Church of Mercy*, he reminds us, once again, that God is always waiting for us to come back and start again:

> Maybe someone among us here is thinking, my sin is so great, I am as far from God as the younger son in the parable, my unbelief is like that of Thomas; I don't have the courage to go back, to believe that God can welcome me and that he is waiting for me, of all people. But God is indeed waiting for you. He asks of you the courage to go to him.
>
> How many times in my pastoral ministry have I heard it said, "Father, I have many sins"; and I have always pleaded: "Don't be afraid, go to him, he is waiting for you, he will take care of everything." We hear many offers from the world around us, but let us take up God's offer instead: his is a caress of love.[57]

Chapter One Reflection Questions

"Socialism" has broad and powerful appeal still today, yet, under socialist regimes in the past century, millions of people have lost both their rights and their lives. What is the reason for its appeal? Why has it not worked in practice?

How were families affected by the Industrial Revolution, for better and for worse?

Pope Leo XIII positively rejected Marx and his socialist ideas because of their adverse effects on the family. In fact, in 1878 he wrote an entire encyclical entitled *Quod Apostolici Muneris* (on socialism) about this. In what ways does Marx's ideology harm the family?

How has divorce affected your life or your family's life? Have you sought healing for any wounds you have suffered or caused?

Alone, the individual is not the bedrock of society. Rather, it is the family that is the foundation of all of society. Why is this so?

With the legalization of same-sex "marriages," we can no longer look at civil and religious marriages as a single entity; the ties between the two have almost completely unraveled. Today, some are calling for a separation of sacramental marriage from civil marriage, as is the practice in Mexico and much of Europe. Others protest this idea, claiming that if Church weddings are separated from the civil sphere, they are worthless. So, where does the Church go from here?

CHAPTER TWO

Back to the Garden

Pius XI, *Casti Connubii*

WARS AND RUMORS OF WARS

Someone once said that all the sins of the world can be traced back to the first three chapters of the Book of Genesis and the Garden of Eden. Without pondering on the happenings that occurred then, it is difficult to understand the heartbreak of the twentieth century. The century didn't start out as a century of violence, social upheaval, and heartbreak. In fact, most people woke up on January 1, 1900, with a song in their hearts. Coloring everything was an energy, an optimism, and a feeling of confidence.

The nineteenth century had changed the world beyond anyone's wildest dreams, and there was every expectation that the twentieth century would "prove to be the best this ever-improving planet had ever seen."[58] But something went terribly wrong, and the twentieth century would prove to be the bloodiest century in history — fulfilling Pope Leo XIII's vision in 1884. There were wars and rumors of wars (see Mt 24:6), including the most insidious war of all, the war on the family.

In this chapter, we will skip over the two popes who followed Pope Leo XIII (Popes Pius X and Benedict XV) and move ahead to the pontificate of Pope Pius XI. Pius XI was pope from 1922 to 1939, during the difficult years between World War I and World War II. The people in his hometown of Desio, Italy, always predicted that Achille Ratti would be pope, and indeed it must have been divine providence, for his path to the papacy was certainly a circuitous one.

An academic and a lover of books, Ratti spent the first years of his priesthood as a seminary professor before moving on to spend the next thirty years working as a librarian — first in the historic Ambrosian Library in Milan and then in the Vatican Library in Rome. He was well into his sixties when, in 1918, Pope Benedict XV asked him to change careers and take a diplomatic post in Poland. Within a period of four years, he went from being a diplomat, to a papal nuncio, to an archbishop, and finally a cardinal. In 1922, Cardinal Achille Ratti was elected pope. He took the name Pius, explaining that he was ordained under Pope Pius IX and it was Pope Pius X who called him to Rome to work in the Vatican library. Furthermore, Pius was a name of peace, and he wanted to dedicate his pontificate to promoting peace in a war-torn world. So, he would be Pope Pius XI, and, by all accounts, he was one of the "greats."

The years following World War I were years of transition and revolution. The sheer loss of life experienced in such a short period of time was something dreadfully new and unprecedented. Consequently, an entire generation was infected with an "eat, drink, and be merry, for tomorrow we die" attitude, which manifested itself in a number of ways.

From the outset, the war had called into question many traditional habits and ways of thinking in Europe and, most especially, in the United States. Sexual themes were increasingly prevalent in media, becoming portrayed more and more regularly in movies, books, and magazines. Sexual behavior changed, and contraception became more technologically sophisticated and socially acceptable. Margaret Sanger was busily promoting "birth control," a term she popularized beginning in 1914.[59] Moreover, "the divorce rate doubled between 1910 and 1928, and it was in the 1920s that no-fault (mutual consent) divorce was brought up for the first time."[60] In fact, "one of the most striking results of the [moral] revolution was a widely pervasive obsession with sex."[61] This was the roaring '20s, after all, the age of speak-easies, dance halls, and a relatively new novelty, the back seat of a car. This "disruption of traditional and conventional customs, manners, and morals left people adrift and struggling to articulate a new code of conduct."[62] This is the world and moral climate that Pope Pius XI inherited on February 6, 1922, the day he was elected pope.

As the twentieth century wore on, the devastating effects of these realities on marriage became painfully apparent. Perhaps the most insidious and far-reaching of the changed social norms was the widespread use and acceptance of contraception. Of course, none of this happened overnight. Honestly, to make sense of it, we need to go back to the late 1700s.

Most people credit Reverend Thomas Malthus, an Anglican cleric and scholar from Great Britain, with starting the modern sexual revolution. In his 1798 "Essay on the Principle of Population," Malthus created the modern "population explosion" scare, saying that "unless it was checked, the population would outgrow food supplies, which would result in mass starvation."[63] He was a strong advocate for family planning, but only through moral means, such as delaying marriage and using sexual self-control.

His proposal struck a cord, as both men and women were increasingly seeking to limit the number of children in their families. No doubt, this desire was accentuated by the shift from an agricultural to an industrial society. Malthus died in 1834, but his population scare outlived him.

In 1839, a new invention by a chemist named Charles Goodyear changed everything: the vulcanization of rubber, which led to the production of cheaper and more effective condoms. Armed with this manufacturing breakthrough, those who wanted to avoid having children found it easier to use condoms, rather than using self-control.

As a matter of fact, "by the turn of the [twentieth] century, the [average] birth rate among white middle-class women had fallen dramatically to two children or less."[64] This was in spite of broad opposition to contraceptives from those in the medical profession, as well as laws banning their sale and distribution. In the United States, Anthony Comstock persuaded Congress in 1873 to legislate against the distribution and sale of contraceptive devices in federal territories. Many states followed suit, and the resulting anti-contraceptive legislation became known as the Comstock laws.[65]

Following closely on the heels of women winning the right to vote in the United States in 1920, Margaret Sanger and others began to wage open war on the Comstock laws. In 1921, Sanger founded the American Birth Control League, working out of an office provided by the American Eugenics Society.

The eugenics movement had grown out of the Malthusian (Malthus) movement. These two movements had much in common, but they differed in that the Malthusians wanted to decrease the total number of people being born, while the eugenics movement mainly wanted to limit the fertility of the poor and the unfit.[66] Specifically, "Eugenics is the belief that some people (the 'unfit') are genetically inferior and should not perpetuate their 'subpar' genes by having children."[67] It is an open secret that Margaret Sanger, the mother of the birth control movement, was a eugenicist.

Sanger, born in 1879 in Corning, New York, "was raised in a stridently socialist, feminist, and atheist home. Her father 'deplored' the Roman Catholic Church."[68] She was the sixth of eleven children, and Margaret believed that so many pregnancies took a toll on her mother's health, contributing to her early death at the age of forty-two. Margaret became a nurse, and the thing that got her out of bed every morning was her unbridled passion for the availability and use of contraceptives. She had her own reasons for choosing to serve the poor and marginalized, but it is safe to say that her writings never indicate any concern for poor children. In 1914, "she launched her publication *The Woman Rebel*, under the masthead, 'No God, No Masters.' The same year, she popularized the phrase, 'birth control.'"[69]

For seven years, Margaret kept her office at the American Eugenics Society, years that included the 1929 stock market crash and the worldwide depression that followed. These events placed great economic, social, and psychological strains on the average family. Millions of people lost their savings as numerous banks collapsed in the early 1930s. During this time, Sanger's ideas became more and more appealing.

Although Sanger had left her original organization over an ideological dispute, the organization eventually reunited in 1939, under the name Birth Control Federation of America. Within a short period of time, the words "birth control" became a public-relations nightmare, and so, in 1942, the organization was renamed the Planned Parenthood Federation of America.[70]

No one can deny the tremendous influence Margaret Sanger had on the practices and moral thinking of her day, and even more so today. The pressures she generated were highly influential in removing the legal, religious, and social barriers to contraception and then abortion. The contraceptionists frequently advocated a whole new concept of marriage.

John F. Kippley, founder of the Couple to Couple League, talks about this in his article "*Casti Connubii*: 60 Years Later, More Relevant Than Ever": "They denied the divine origin and the permanence of marriage and made efficient contraception the technological cornerstone of 'companionate' marriage — a serial polygamy consisting of legal marriage, efficient contraception, divorce when boredom set in, and then remarriage to start the process over."[71]

Eventually, the Comstock law was repealed. Even so, to finally succeed in her march to legalize birth control, Margaret Sanger needed to focus on a larger and more influential enemy. The Catholic Church fit the bill perfectly. In an article entitled "Sanger's Victory," Allan Carlson, president of the Howard Center for Family, Religion & Society confirms this:

> Opposition to Catholicism suited Sanger personally. Her father had tutored her on the presumed evils and dangers of Rome. Moreover, her study of and involvement in socialist activities before the war had taught her the value of a clearly identified foe when launching a social-political movement. Already marginalized in American life, Catholics were the obvious choice. In her desire to gain a sacred canopy for birth control, she could easily play on four-century-old [hostilities] between Protestants and Catholics to bring the former to her side.[72]

Here it is interesting to note that for four hundred years after the Protestant Reformation in the sixteenth century, birth control was never seen as a Catholic versus Protestant issue. As a matter of fact, the Comstock laws were essentially passed by Protestant legislatures for a basically Protestant America.

Few people realize that up until 1930, "*all* Protestant denominations agreed with the Catholic Church's teaching condemning contraception as sinful."[73] However, at its 1930 Lambeth Conference,[74] the Anglican church, swayed by growing social pressure from Margaret Sanger and others, announced that contraception would be allowed in *some* circumstances:

> Where there is a clearly felt moral obligation to limit or avoid parenthood, the method must be decided on Christian principles. The primary and obvious method is complete abstinence from intercourse (as far as may be necessary) in a life of discipleship and self-control lived in the pow-

er of the Holy Spirit. Nevertheless, in those cases where there is such a clearly felt moral obligation to limit or avoid parenthood, and where there is a morally sound reason for avoiding complete abstinence, *the Conference agrees that other methods may be used, provided that this is done in the light of the same Christian principles.* The Conference records its strong condemnation of the use of any methods of conception-control for motives of selfishness, luxury, or mere convenience.[75]

The Anglican bishops reluctantly accepted marital contraception as morally licit without even elaborating on what they meant by "Christian principles." In spite of this, they could not hide from the fact that, in previous years, they had always taught that marital contraception was immoral, as evidenced in this statement from the 1920 Lambeth Conference: "We utter an *emphatic warning against the use of unnatural means for the avoidance of conception,* together with the grave dangers — physical, moral, and religious — thereby incurred, and against the evils with which the extension of such use threatens the race."[76]

These statements from the 1920 and 1930 Lambeth Conferences show how quickly the culture had changed in just ten years. In fact, soon after the 1930 Lambeth Conference, the Anglican Communion completely caved in, allowing contraception across the board. "Since then, all other Protestant denominations have followed suit. Today, the Catholic Church alone proclaims the historic Christian position on contraception."[77]

This sudden change in Anglican teaching was so upsetting to Pope Pius XI that he responded by writing his encyclical letter *Casti Connubii* ("Of Chaste Marriage"), which was released on December 31, 1930, just four months after the Lambeth Conference. "Those who had thought Pius XI was only a dry historian were surprised to discover that the passionate tone of the encyclical revealed the heart of a true father of peoples, a priest, a human being, full of feeling and love for mankind."[78]

The document covers a wide range of topics concerning Christian marriage and reproductive rights, and in doing so it gives us an interesting window into the Church's perception of the social and religious situation surrounding marriage and procreation at the time. *Casti Connubii*, which describes point by point the characteristics of a Christian marriage, is perhaps the Church's most complete teaching on the subject of Christian marriage.

Pope Pius XI was a serious man, this was a serious time, and, as we will see, this is a serious document. Responding to the Anglican resolution at Lambeth, Pope Pius spoke forcefully and in no uncertain terms about the Church's unchanged position on contraception:

> Since, therefore, openly departing from the uninterrupted Christian tradition some recently have judged it possible solemnly to declare another doctrine regarding this question, the Catholic Church, to whom God has entrusted the defense of the integrity and purity of morals, standing erect in the midst of the moral ruin which surrounds her, in order that she may preserve the chastity of the nuptial union from being defiled by this foul stain, raises her voice in token of her divine ambassadorship and through Our mouth proclaims anew: any use whatsoever of matrimony exercised in such a way that the act is deliberately frustrated in its natural power to generate life is an offense against the law of God and of nature, and those who indulge in such are branded with the guilt of a grave sin.[79]

Not only did the pope confirm the Church's perennial teaching about contraception, he offered a sobering reminder to all of us that it is precisely because of our "human tendency to rationalize our private [choices] that Christ established a teaching Church. It is the Church, and not private judgment, that has been entrusted with revelation regarding faith and morals."[80]

CASTI CONNUBII

Casti Connubii is the second in a trilogy of three major encyclicals on marriage and family life, used to "restate and strengthen the Church's teaching."[81] The first was Pope Leo XIII's 1880 encyclical, *Arcanum*, on Christian marriage; the second was Pope Pius XI's 1930 encyclical on chaste marriage, *Casti Connubii*; and the third was Pope Paul VI's 1968 definitive teaching on contraception and human life, *Humanae Vitae*. All of these documents were written to counter a perceived threat to marriage. "In each of these encyclicals, the Church not only restates its perennial teaching on marriage and family, but also develops aspects of the theology of marriage that had not been fully articulated before."[82]

What Is Marriage?

We remember from our review of Pope Leo XIII's encyclical *Arcanum* that he put it in its proper context by asking the question, "What did God intend?" In a similar way, Pope Pius XI began *Casti Connubii* by symbolically asking, "What is marriage?" It is a fair question, particularly in our day and age. Today, the true meaning of marriage frequently gets lost between the wedding invitations and the parties, so the Church wants to make sure that we know the answer to this question.

 Casti Connubii reaffirms the main points found in *Arcanum*, particularly pertaining to the sacramental nature of marriage and the evils of divorce. Just by asking the question, "What is marriage?" Pius XI expanded his teaching into some other areas. Drawing from the teachings of Saint Augustine, there are three precepts of marriage: the begetting and education of children, the fidelity of the spouses, and the graces of the sacrament.

The encyclical begins by reminding us that marriage is "of its very nature"[83] a divine institution. God instituted marriage, but no one is obliged to marry. However, once a couple does enter matrimony, they do it on God's terms, not their own.[84] In other words, "a man and a woman can enter into the married state — *but they have no freedom as to what that state is*. They can do well or ill. But they can't change what the *plan* is."[85] According to Pope Pius: "This freedom ... regards only the question whether the contracting parties really wish to enter upon matrimony or to marry this particular person; but the nature of matrimony is entirely independent of the free will of man, so that if one has once contracted matrimony, he is thereby subject to its divinely made laws and its essential properties."[86]

Contrary to popular opinion, the "main union of marriage is not the physical. It is, rather, the spiritual union of the hearts and minds of the married couple."[87] The fact that marriage goes far beyond the physical relationship of the partners is what separates us from the animals. No union on earth is as intimate as marriage. We see this particularly in times of need, when there is a real demand upon the spiritual resources of the couple, which can only come from a depth of understanding between the husband and wife.

If a marriage is based on passion alone, the risk for failure is great. As we can well appreciate, our passions burn out, and our physical bodies change as the years go by. Spiritual qualities are more enduring than the physical, and it is upon these spiritual qualities that an enduring union must be founded:

> By matrimony, therefore, the souls of the contracting parties are joined and knit together more directly and more intimately than are their bodies, and that not by any passing affection of sense of spirit, but by a deliberate and firm act of the will; and from this

union of souls by God's decree, a sacred and invio-
lable bond arises. Hence the nature of this contract,
which is proper and peculiar to it alone, makes it
entirely different both from the union of animals
entered into by the blind instinct of nature alone
in which neither reason nor free will plays a part,
and also from the haphazard unions of men, which
are far removed from all true and honorable unions
of will and enjoy none of the rights of family life.[88]

Christian marriage is a partnership between a husband and
wife, with God as the third partner. It should be rooted in unselfish love, which is exactly how God loves us. Since procreation
and education of children is the first precept of marriage, married couples are, in fact, co-creators of the universe. Together with
God, they keep the human race in existence. Failing in marriage,
therefore, means failing God, our partner.

Because marriage was designed specifically for the creation of
children, their education must also be the priority in any marriage. We are all created to know, love, and serve God, and parents have the responsibility to help their children along this path.
From the beginning, parents must help develop deep faith and
virtue in their children:

> Thus amongst the blessings of marriage, the child
> holds the first place. And indeed, the Creator of the
> human race himself, Who in His goodness wishes
> to use men as His helpers in the propagation of life,
> taught this when, instituting marriage in Paradise,
> He said to our first parents, and through them to
> all future spouses: "Increase and multiply, and fill
> the earth."[89]
>
> The blessing of offspring, however, is not com-
> pleted by the mere begetting of them, but some-

thing else must be added, namely the proper education of the offspring. For no one can fail to see
that children are incapable of providing wholly
for themselves, even in matters pertaining to their
natural life, and much less in those pertaining to
the supernatural, but require for many years to be
helped, instructed, and educated by others.[90]

To have a marriage that embraces children (the first precept
of marriage), there must be fidelity and dedication of the spouses
to each other (the second precept). Real fidelity is centered in an
abiding "union of mind and heart."[91] Hence, "if internal union is
protected, there will never be any reason for worry about external
fidelity."[92]

In other words, if a husband and wife strive to be faithful to
each other through their thoughts and actions, there is very little
chance that either will be unfaithful. (On this point, Pope Pius
discouraged both husband and wife from spending too much time
with other people of the opposite sex.)

Fidelity is the fruit of mutual love, which is one of the blessings of a Christian marriage. This kind of love puts the needs
and cares of the other person first. When a husband loves his
wife, he seeks what is good for her, and a wife should do the
same for her husband. And the greatest goods are not physical,
but spiritual:

The love, then, of which we are speaking is not that
based on the passing lust of the moment nor does
it consist in pleasing words only, but in the deep
attachment of the heart which is expressed in action, since love is proved by deeds. This outward
expression of love in the home demands not only
mutual help but must go further; must have as its
primary purpose that man and wife help each other

day by day in forming and perfecting themselves in
the interior life, so that through their partnership in
life they may advance ever more and more in virtue, and above all that they may grow in true love
toward God and their neighbor.[93]

The mutual love of the spouses should prevent either party
from dominating the other, for true love is always seeking the
good of both:

"For matrimonial faith demands that husband and
wife be joined in an especially holy and pure love,
not as adulterers love each other, but as Christ
loved the Church. This precept the Apostle laid
down when he said: 'Husbands, love your wives as
Christ also loved the Church' ... [which] He embraced with a boundless love not for the sake of His
own advantage, but seeking only the good of His
Spouse."[94]

Here Pius XI echoed the words of Leo XIII in dealing with the
issues of unity and indissolubility of marriage. When Our Lord
said: "'Now they are no longer two, but one flesh. What therefore
God has joined together, let no man put asunder,' (Matt 19:6), He
was reserving for God alone the power [to dissolve] a marriage,
which is a sacrament and has also been perfected by marital intercourse."[95] We know from the Church's teaching that marriage
cannot be dissolved by any human being. Consequently, Catholics know that they are with their partners until death, which is
motivation enough to do the best they can to make their marriage
succeed.

The third precept of marriage is that it is a sacrament, which
means it is a source of divine grace. When the spouses utter their
marriage vows before a priest or deacon, they are, in fact, minis-

tering the sacrament to each other. In doing so, they are bestowing Christ's sanctifying grace on one another.[96]

In a sacramental marriage, the spouses are also given special gifts to navigate the ups and downs of life, which might otherwise seem impossible. As the pope expressed it:

> By the very fact, therefore, that the faithful with sincere mind give such consent, they open up for themselves a treasure of sacramental grace from which they draw supernatural power for the fulfilling of their rights and duties faithfully, holily, perseveringly even unto death. Hence this sacrament not only increases sanctifying grace … but also adds particular gifts, dispositions, seeds of grace, by elevating and perfecting the natural powers. By these gifts the parties are assisted not only in understanding, but in knowing intimately, in adhering to firmly, in willing effectively, and in successfully putting into practice, those things which pertain to the marriage state.[97]

What Are the Threats to Marriage?

To preserve marriage, it is important to recognize clearly those things that are detrimental to Christian marriage. First among Pope Pius's concerns were various cultural issues in his time, all of which are still far too familiar to us. The pope was particularly scandalized by the entertainment industry with its salacious anti-marriage propaganda, as seen in books, plays, movies, newspapers, and even in the popular songs of the day.

Moreover, he was troubled that so many people (Catholic and non-Catholic) deny that God is the author of marriage, believing that it is simply another human institution. Other major obstacles to healthy, holy marriages were selfishness, cohabitation, and the humiliation of one spouse by the other. As the pope pointed out, none of this is rooted in mutual love.

There are also many vices opposed to Christian marriage, including contraception, abortion, sterilization, adultery, false liberty, and divorce. Following the lead of Pope Leo XIII, Pius also addressed the problems that can come from marrying a non-Catholic.

For our purposes, it is important to look at what the pope had to say about the use of contraception in marriage, which is what prompted him to write *Casti Connubii* in the first place. Recall that up until the Lambeth Conference in 1930, when the Anglican bishops broke with tradition, all Christian churches taught that using any kind of contraception was intrinsically evil.

On this point, the pope was exceptionally clear. Contraception is wrong, and no matter what, nothing good can come from an intrinsically evil act. In other words, "neither the intention of the one acting nor the circumstances have anything to do with making an intrinsically evil act good."[98]

This is why contraception may not be used to prevent the conception of a child under any circumstances. Pope Pius specifically underscored this important Church teaching:

> First consideration is due to the offspring, which many have the boldness to call the disagreeable burden of matrimony and which they say is to be carefully avoided by married people not through virtuous continence ... but by frustrating the marriage act. Some justify this criminal abuse on the ground that they are weary of children and wish to gratify their desires without their consequent burden. Others say that they cannot on one hand remain continent nor on the other hand can they have children because of the difficulties whether on the part of the mother or on the part of family circumstances.[99]

And:

> But no reason, however grave, may be put forward
> by which anything intrinsically against nature may
> become conformable to nature and morally good.
> Since, therefore, the [marital] act is destined pri-
> marily by nature for the begetting of children, those
> who in exercising it deliberately frustrate its natural
> power and purpose sin against nature and commit a
> deed which is shameful and intrinsically vicious.[100]

These were strong words, on such a controversial issue, and
they were not well received by those involved in the birth control
movement. Sanger took aim at the pope's remarks in no uncertain terms. It took her exactly two weeks to issue a long public
response, of which this is just a small selection:

> The steady advance of the birth control movement
> can only receive fresh impetus from the new inter-
> est which has been aroused by the attack of Pope
> Pius XI.
>
> His encyclical letter, "Of Chaste Marriage," made
> public in January, 1931, aims to regulate the conju-
> gal affairs of Catholic men and women, without the
> benefit of science, and according to theories written
> by St. Augustine, also a bachelor, who died fifteen
> centuries ago. The Pope makes it perfectly plain that
> Catholics are expected to give up health, happiness,
> and life itself while making every other conceivable
> sacrifice rather than to have dominion over nature's
> processes of procreation. His letter denies that any
> claims of poverty, sickness, or other hindrances to
> proper rearing of children are valid reasons for the
> scientific limitation of offspring. As for the breeding

of criminal, diseased, feeble-minded, and insane classes, the Pope opposes every method of control except that of suggesting to these unfortunate people to please not do it any more.

One must deplore the fact that Pope Pius should have chosen this time of the world's distress from unemployment, poverty, and economic maladjustment to advertise doctrines and advise conduct which can only tend to aggravate that distress.[101]

Certainly, for some people, having the number of children that God decides can indeed be a great stress, both physically and economically. But God is ever present, and "it seems clear that if men live so as to serve God wholeheartedly, He will take care that their human nature serves, rather than masters them. And in those rare cases when God permits a situation which calls for heroism, He will be plentiful with His graces to enable His servants to face the problem as they should."[102]

Pope Pius XI concluded *Casti Connubii* by asking the faithful to spread these teachings far and wide. He wanted the encyclical to be accompanied by sound instruction "so that Catholics everywhere may come to a full knowledge of the Church's doctrine on the [Sacrament of Matrimony]."[103] However, learning is not enough. His greatest wish was for the faithful to fall in love with the beauty of Christian marriage, as defined by the Church, and in doing so to make it their own.

Chapter Two Reflection Questions

How can it be that Margaret Sanger, a well-known eugenicist, is still revered around the world? What is at the root of this kind of thinking?

What is authentic freedom? How might the Church's teachings on contraception be an affirmation of our personal freedom, rather than a hindrance to us?

Pope Pius XI sets the tone early in this document by telling us that the spiritual union of the spouses is more important and more intimate than the physical. Why is it so important to understand this, particularly today?

Reflect on the pope's comments that nothing good can come from an evil act. He is obviously talking about using contraception. However, think of the many other areas in your life where this also applies.

What jumped out at you when you read that short passage of Margaret Sanger's reply to the pope's encyclical?

CHAPTER THREE

Searching for Truth

Paul VI, *Humanae Vitae*

UNCERTAIN TIMES

It is probably fair to ask, as did the editors of *America* magazine in a 2014 article, "Has *any* pope reigned over a more volatile age than Giovanni Battista Montini?"[104] The pontificate of Pope Paul VI occurred during the upheaval of the 1960s and the uncertainty of the 1970s, a time when the whole world, most particularly the West, was in moral chaos. When Cardinal Montini was elected to the papacy on June 21, 1963, few realized the "convulsions that would wrench both Church and world in the next decade."[105]

Paul VI was born Giovanni Battista Montini on September 26, 1897, in the province of Brescia, Italy. A sickly child, he had a love for learning and was devoted to his Catholic faith. He entered the seminary at the tender age of nineteen and was ordained a priest on May 29, 1920, just twenty-three years old. Later in his priesthood, he would work closely with Pope Pius XII as he guided the Church before and after the World War II, and he remained fiercely loyal to him throughout his life, even opening the cause for his canonization, along with that of Pope John XXIII, on November 18, 1965, during the last session of the Second Vatican Council.

To make sense of Paul, the man, the pope, and his encyclical *Humanae Vitae* ("Of Human Life"), we need to look at him through the lens of the Second Vatican Council (more commonly known today as Vatican II). Paul VI inherited this council from his predecessor, Pope John XXIII, who opened it on October 11, 1962. On December 8, 1965, Pope Paul VI brought the council to a successful close, and then he suffered through thirteen years of conflict over its implementation, once calling it a "hornet's nest."[106]

Historians have called the council the most important Catholic event of the twentieth century. With 2,860 bishops in attendance, it was the largest ecumenical council ever held. Providing a sense of what the council accomplished was its output: "The council fathers' main achievement can be seen in the 16 documents they adopted by overwhelming majorities.... They deal with the Church, the Church in the modern world, liturgy, and divine revelation."[107]

The years leading up to and following the council were rocked by unprecedented social challenges, both globally and at home. The Cold War, the Korean War, the Vietnam War, the Cuban Missile Crisis, the feminist movement, the civil rights movement, and the birth control movement all affected the human psyche. Added to this were the "historic revolutions taking place in technology, science, politics, economics, and culture."[108]

People from around the world struggled to make sense of it all. Their internal ache expressed itself in a number of ways, primarily in various forms of secularism, materialism, moral relativism, and individualism. The brutalities of the twentieth century had clearly demonstrated what could happen in the name of progress and development when God is excluded.[109] In fact, people wondered if a "Church that was so old, that had been there all along the way and evidently did not prevent the unprecedented assaults on human dignity of the twentieth century, [could] make a credible case that it has something positive to offer?"[110]

John XXIII certainly thought so. He used to say, "The world has its problems, for which it anxiously seeks a solution,"[111] and he was positive that the Church could help provide that solution. This was the impetus for Vatican II. In his mind, this modern council would reaffirm all of the Church's teachings, but in a new and updated way, so that the contemporary world could hear the Good News of Jesus Christ. In other words, he wanted this to be a *pastoral* council.

Pope John's greatest concern was that the sacred deposit of Christian doctrine be guarded and taught more effectively.[112] And it was important to him that the Church's doctrine be presented in a positive way. As George Weigel explains in his masterpiece, *Witness to Hope: The Biography of Pope John Paul II*, John XXIII "envisioned an open conversation in which the world's bishops would relive the experience of Christ's apostles at Pentecost. The Second Vatican Council, in the Pope's mind, would renew Christian faith as a vibrant way of life; it would engage modernity in dialogue; it would issue no condemnations; it would try to give voice again to the pure message of the Gospel. It would, in the now-famous phrase, 'open the Church's windows to the modern world.'"[113]

If only it had been that easy. Sadly, as Weigel notes, "The Church itself was deeply divided about the possibility of a serious dialogue with modernity."[114] Some senior members of the Church, particularly in areas where the Church was persecuted, worried that such a dialogue would inevitably lead to the fall of Christianity.

Others believed, just as passionately, "that the Church's vision of human dignity and human destiny could help direct the modern quest for freedom into productive rather than destructive channels."[115] And there were still others who just wanted change, because, after all, this was the 1960s, and change was the order of the day.

This had all the makings of a real drama, and in light of this, Vatican II became a worldwide curiosity. "Throughout 1962–65, there were two places and events in the world where foreign correspondents knew their story would get top billing — the Viet-

nam War and the Second Vatican Council. Reporters flocked to
Rome because it was safer than Vietnam."[116] Their presence alone
had an incredible influence on the council. Actually, the media
itself became part of the story. This is how the late American theologian, Father Matthew Lamb, who was studying in Rome at the
time, explained the scenario: "[The correspondents] didn't understand theology and what to do. [Consequently,] they started using
political categories. By the second session, it was 'conservative' vs.
'liberal' — it was who was winning."[117]

At one of the press conferences, Father Lamb observed that an
American theologian "would explain in serious detail for 20 minutes what had been debated that morning, and then a priest, who
was considered a leading British theologian, would get up and tell
the media representatives that it was quite simple: 'liberal vs. conservative.'"[118] The press would invariably quote those priests from
around the world who fell into the liberal template or camp.[119]

Later, Father Lamb claimed "that 95 [percent] of Catholics, including religious and priests, didn't study the documents of the
Council ... they were reading the press reports in the mainstream
media. And the diocesan papers would pick those reports up,
too."[120]

Years later, Pope Emeritus Benedict XVI would concur with
Father Lamb's assessment a few days after his February 11, 2013,
resignation:

> There was a Council of the fathers — the true
> Council — but there was also the Council of the
> media. It was almost a Council unto itself, and the
> world perceived the Council through the media.
> Therefore, the Council that immediately and effi-
> ciently arrived to the people was that of the media,
> not that of the fathers.
>
> We know that this Council of the media was
> accessible to all. Therefore, this was the dominant,

more efficient one and has created so much calamity, so many problems, really so much misery — seminaries closed; convents closed; liturgy trivialized.[121]

Pope John XXIII died on June 3, 1963, between the first and second sessions of the council. Less than three weeks later, on June 21, 1963, the cardinals chose Giovanni Battista Montini to be John's successor. He chose the name Paul because, like Saint Paul, he wanted to preach the Gospel to the ends of the earth.[122]

Pope Paul VI went on to visit six continents, more than any of his predecessors. It has been said that he "was a missionary, a reformer, an upholder of tradition, and on a personal level, someone who had a profound understanding of the priesthood, and the theology of the Cross."[123] In the end, however, Pope Paul's mission territory turned out to be in his own backyard, inside the Church.

> When John XXIII died in 1963, Pope Paul could have tried to slow Vatican II, or even halted it altogether. But wisely — and providentially, Father Langlois believes — Paul gave his full backing to Blessed John's Council, and shepherded all its decrees and documents to their conclusion. For doing so, he was criticized by both the Left and Right, the former claiming he didn't go nearly as far as he should, the latter saying he was much too progressive. Neither of the critics are correct says Father Langlois. "If you actually examine the documents carefully, there is nothing in them that sustains either reactionary thinking, or a revolutionary agenda."[124]

Pope Paul VI possessed the gift of mediation. He well understood the importance of dialogue, once claiming that dialogue was the new word for charity.[125] Because of this, he was able to guide the council through three tumultuous sessions. And he was able to lead the bishops to the point of obtaining near-unanimity on all documents, curbing both conservative and overly innovative tendencies. A contemporary of his once remarked, "Never have I met anyone who had to say so little to establish his authority."[126]

Even so, those years were indeed a time of suffering for him. He had watched many disillusioned lay people leave the Church. Similarly, thousands of priests and religious left the religious life before, during, and after Vatican II, and although the reasons were many, Pope Paul VI was frequently blamed. "The virus of dissent … spread rapidly and, with media support, soon became entrenched. The 'smoke of Satan,' Paul famously said, had seeped into the Church."[127] On the last day of the council, he wrote: "Perhaps God called me and keeps me in his service, not so much because I had a certain attitude toward him, or because through me he governs and saves the Church from its present difficulties, but because I suffer for the Church, and it is clear that it is He, not others, who guides it and saves it."[128]

Underneath all of this, however, there was something more serious brewing that would change everything — for the pope and the entire Church. The birth control pill, for which Margaret Sanger and her companions had fought so hard, had come on the market in 1960. Sanger's dream had come true: She frequently said that she wanted a contraceptive pill that was as "easy to take as an aspirin."[129] Almost overnight, it became a cultural phenomenon, as more and more women (Catholic and not) gained access to this new drug.

Most people just assumed that the Second Vatican Council would deal with the birth control issue. However, in 1963, not long before his death, Pope John XXIII took the matter out of the council's hands and turned it over to a new Papal Commission for the Study of Problems of Population, Family, and Birthrate. This commission, later reappointed by Paul VI, "was to advise [Paul] on the tangle of issues indicated in its title."[130] Most people referred to it as the "birth control commission," and to them the only issue at stake was whether or not Catholics would be allowed to take the pill.

Under John XXIII, the commission had six members, but when Paul VI became pope, he increased the size to seventy-two, which included cardinals, bishops, theologians, physicians, and married people. The specific question that he asked the commission to study was whether a newly discovered technique for preventing conception — the birth control pill — was considered contraception? Jesuit scholar Father Peter F. Ryan unpacks this question:

> "Previously, conception could be prevented only by interfering with a couple's outward behavior during intercourse, for example, through withdrawal or the use of a condom. Since the pill is not taken at the time of intercourse and therefore does not affect the couple's behavior, the question arose as to whether the use of the pill was included in what the Church condemns."[131]

Some have claimed that the pope himself may have doubted the Church's position when he asked the commission to take up this question. There is no evidence to suggest this. Rather, Pope Paul was eager to help married couples in any way he could, and he did not want to condemn anything the tradition did not require him to condemn.[132] In reality, he was open to being convinced that a development consistent with the Church's long tradition allowed the use of the pill. According to Father Ryan:

> Paul VI was thinking both traditionally and pastorally. He knew he had to teach the truth that the Church had always taught, but in order not to burden people unnecessarily, he wanted to be sure not to teach what was not required by the tradition.

> He therefore had theologians look into the matter
> to see if they had arguments that could convince
> him that the moral truth he had to teach about the
> wrongness of contraception left any wiggle room
> for the use of the pill. They did not convince him.[133]

The nearly unanimous conclusion of the commission was that the pill was, undeniably, contraceptive. When their work was completed, however, "the commission was divided between a majority that argued for a change in the classic Catholic position that contraception was immoral, and a minority that wanted to affirm that teaching."[134] The commission had changed the question from whether the use of the pill violated Church teaching to whether the Church's teaching against contraception was justified!

Those in the majority sent their findings, eventually dubbed the "Majority Report," to Pope Paul in June 1966. They argued that "[marital] morality should be measured by 'the totality of married life,' rather than by the openness of each act of intercourse to conception."[135] In essence, the Majority Report argued that a couple could use contraception if they had sufficient reason and if they were open to life over the "totality" of their marriage. A "Minority Report" was also submitted to the pope, which argued that the Church's constant and consistent teaching should be maintained.

The pope agreed with the findings of the commission regarding the birth control pill being contraceptive, but he disagreed with the majority's proposal that the Church's teaching on contraception should be changed. Instead, Father Ryan explains that the pope reaffirmed the Church's position on this issue.

> Of special significance is his definition of contra-
> ception, which makes it clear that what is relevant
> is not the behavior involved but the intention to
> impede, no matter how that intention is carried
> out. The pope thus indicates that the Church's con-

demnation of contraception extends to the pill, for
he excludes as morally wrong "any action which
either before, at the moment of, or after sexual intercourse, is specifically intended to prevent procreation — whether as an end or as a means."[136]

In the end, Pope Paul thanked the commission for its work but
"pointed out that nothing it said could relieve him, the supreme
teacher of the Church, of his 'duty of deciding' the question."[137]
Even though a majority voted to change Church teaching, he
could not overlook the fact that contraception in any form is intrinsically evil. It appears only Pope Paul VI and a handful of others understood that truth, not numbers, was what really mattered.

The commission finished its work in 1966, and it produced
three documents, which were neither authoritative nor binding
on the pope, nor were they meant for public release. Despite this,
portions of the three documents were leaked to the press in 1967
and were published in *the Tablet*, a Catholic weekly published in
London, and the *National Catholic Reporter*, which is published
in the United States. No doubt, this was to put pressure on the
pope to make a decision, as the leaks expressed the views of the
"majority" of the commission.

Meanwhile, Pope Paul VI studied the arguments put forth by
the commission, and he prayed and prayed. Some say he prayed
too long, for it took him more than two years to issue the encyclical *Humanae Vitae*, which was his response to the commission's
recommendation. As the months and years passed between the
commission's findings and the pope's decision, more and more
people began to speculate that change was a done deal. In fact:

> Some theologians were saying that because the
> teaching had been questioned, and because there
> were theologians who thought it was morally ac-
> ceptable to practice contraception, and because

time had passed and the Church had not condemned that view, one can take that view as a
probable opinion and apply it. Such claims were
not without their effect on the pastoral life of the
Church. When months passed and Paul VI was not
saying anything — and it was not clear whether he
ever would — many pastors began to pass that advice on.[138]

It was within this context that *Humanae Vitae* was finally published on July 25, 1968. The pope lived another ten years, and
although he continued his teaching by using other forms of communication, *Humanae Vitae* was the last encyclical he ever wrote.
The promulgation of this encyclical was perhaps the loneliest moment of Pope Paul VI's pontificate. After its release, he was fero-
ciously attacked and criticized — both from within the Church
and from those on the outside — for not liberalizing the Church's
teaching on contraception.

His faith sustained him: "He knew, as long as he retained that,
nothing in this life could cause permanent damage, no matter how
bad any situation became."[139] When asked about this, he said: "I
have never felt the weight of my office as in this situation. I have
studied, read, and discussed as much as possible; and I have also
prayed very much."[140]

Pope Paul VI died on August 6, 1978, on the feast of the Trans-
figuration of Jesus. He was beatified on October 19, 2014. Pope
Francis schedule him to be canonized in October 2018.

HUMANAE VITAE

Humanae Vitae is the third in a trilogy of three major encyclicals on marriage and family life, which build on one another,
while also restating and strengthening the Church's teaching.[141]
In the previous two chapters, we considered the encyclicals in
light of specific questions: "What did God intend?" and "What is

marriage?" Reading *Humanae Vitae*, the question we should ask (along with Pope Paul VI) is, "What is truth?"

In spite of the uproar connected with *Humanae Vitae*, it is not a lengthy treatise. In fact, it is very short, containing only thirty-one articles. Initially, the tone of the encyclical is one of sadness, almost reluctance. It then gives way to a calm confidence, which manifests the truth of its message. As Dr. Ralph McInerny expresses it, "Paul knows the hardness of his teaching, but he also knows that it is not his, but God's."[142]

Paul VI addressed this encyclical letter not only to bishops, priests, and all of the faithful, but also to "all men of good will." By doing this, he reminded the Church and the world that truth is truth, and that it is accessible and applicable to all. Reasonable people in search of the truth can come to an understanding and acceptance of the Church's teachings on the regulation of birth because these teachings are not the creation of the Catholic Church, but come from the Creator — the Source of all Truth. With this in mind, he sets the stage for the entire encyclical:

> The transmission of human life is a most serious role in which married people collaborate freely and responsibly with God the Creator. It has always been a source of great joy to them, even though it sometimes entails many difficulties and hardships.
>
> The fulfillment of this duty has always posed problems to the conscience of married people, but the recent course of human society and the concomitant changes have provoked new questions. The Church cannot ignore these questions, for they concern matters intimately connected with the life and happiness of human beings.[143]

Problem and Competency of the Magisterium

Not surprisingly, the letter begins by pointing to the teaching of

Paul VI's predecessors, reminding us that married persons have the "most serious role" of transmitting human life as free and responsible collaborators of God the Creator.[144] In other words, a newly conceived child is not only man's creation, he or she is the result of the collaboration between man, woman, and God. The word collaborators is an important reminder that the transmission of life cannot be debated, decided, or even understood apart from God and his design.

Being a parent is not easy, and Paul VI recognized and acknowledged this. He also recognized that married couples have always faced questions concerning their duty of transmitting human life, and that these questions — a matter of life and death, and therefore urgent — were becoming more pressing in the modern age. When Paul VI wrote *Humanae Vitae*, people were increasingly questioning overpopulation, the difficulty of educating a large number of children, and the changing role of women in society and its effect on a couple's marital relationship.

Yet the issue that stands at the heart of *Humanae Vitae* is man's newfound desire to control every aspect of his life:

> The most remarkable development of all is to be seen in man's stupendous progress in the domination and rational organization of the forces of nature to the point that he is endeavoring to extend this control over every aspect of his own life — over his body, over his mind and emotions, over his social life, and even over the laws that regulate the transmission of life.[145]

Without using the exact phrase, Paul VI described the "contraceptive mentality" that has taken hold of our world today. This mentality expresses itself in wanting and needing to control everything. In effect, Paul VI was asking the question: Just because a woman can now take a pill to control her fertility, should she?

Many have proposed that it is an intelligent use of human reason for a woman to use contraception to control the biological processes of her body. The Church disagrees, claiming that just because something is technically possible does not make it morally permissible. God endowed both men and women with great freedom, but freedom is naturally linked with responsibility. We are free to take responsibility for our own actions.

Those on the commission who signed the Majority Report did so on the basis of what is called the "principle of totality." The principle of totality was a relatively new development in moral theology during the 1960s, and it was gaining followers among dissenting theologians of the day. In essence, this principle denies there are moral absolutes; in other words, there is nothing that is and always will be an intrinsically evil act.

A proponent of this principle would argue that a married couple may use contraception to postpone pregnancy if they have a legitimate reason to do so. According to this rationale, the moral judgment of the use of contraception should not be based on one single act of intercourse or even subsequent individual acts, but rather on the totality of non-contraceptive acts within marriage.

Despite those who would advocate for "the principle of totality," the Church's teachings on marriage are "based on the natural law as illuminated and enriched by divine Revelation."[146] This natural law is the law written on the heart of each man and woman, which enables us to discern good and evil. While the application of the natural law can vary greatly according to the various conditions of life — that is, places, times, circumstances, and even among the diversity of cultures — it remains a rule that binds people together and imposes common principles upon them.[147] Therefore, even when customs and ideas change, the natural law remains unchangeable; its principles, even if they are rejected, cannot be removed from the heart of man and woman.[148]

This is where the teaching authority of the Church is so important. Christ granted the Church the ability to interpret the natural law: "Jesus Christ, when He communicated His divine power to Peter and the other Apostles and sent them to teach all nations His commandments, constituted them as the authentic guardians and interpreters of the whole moral law, not only, that is, of the law of the Gospel but also of the natural law."[149] Consequently, we can trust that the teaching of the pope and the bishops united with him is authentic, for they are teachers endowed with the authority of Christ.

A "Total Vision of Man"

Part II of *Humanae Vitae* discusses some of the more demanding issues of our day. In particular, Paul VI addressed what it means to be human, marital love, responsible parenthood, the nature and purpose of the marital act and its two inseparable aspects (union and procreation), and the illicit and licit means of regulating births. He also issued a prophetic warning regarding the consequences of widespread contraception, which we will look at in more depth shortly.

Looking back on the events of the twentieth century, Pope Paul VI, along with the council fathers, realized that what was missing in the world was a correct understanding of what it means to be human. He wanted to present a total vision of man, "the whole man":[150]

> The question of human procreation, like every other question which touches human life, involves more than the limited aspects specific to such disciplines as biology, psychology, demography or sociology. It is the whole man and the whole mission to which he is called that must be considered: both its natural, earthly aspects and its supernatural, eternal aspects.[151]

The decision to use contraception needs to be considered in

light of our earthly life, as well as our eternal life. Because we are made in the image and likeness of God, we are integrated beings, a union of body and soul. In light of this, we should always remember that our actions have eternal consequences. Our goal in this life is to prepare for eternity with God. In other words, what we do to our body, we also do to our souls.

Pope Paul VI's integrated vision of the human person is crucial to understanding and accepting the Church's teaching on contraception. It is easy to misunderstand the Church's teaching if we view it with only a partial understanding of the human person. For example, evaluating this teaching simply in light of the human person's freedom to exercise his will might easily lead to the conclusion that the Church's teaching is unnecessarily restrictive.

It is also important to understand the true concept of marital love and responsible parenthood, if we want to understand the Church's teachings on marriage, sex, and contraception. This is especially important because at the time of the promulgation of *Humanae Vitae*, many were citing the demands of marital love and responsible parenthood as justification for a change in Church teaching. As Paul VI pointed out, marital love, a love that unites husband and wife in an intimate communion of persons, is life-giving. God, who is love, has made man and woman in his image and likeness, and he calls each of them to a vocation to love — a selfless giving of oneself to another. This type of love is not only fruitful, it goes "beyond this to bring new life into being."[152]

When Paul VI wrote *Humanae Vitae*, many were insisting that couples be "responsible" in their parenthood, and they believed that contraception could be an aid in that. The pope acknowledged that the insistence on "responsible" parenthood was correct; however, responsible parenthood must be correctly understood. Responsible parenthood requires that we have an intimate knowledge of our own "biological processes."[153]

Men and women are endowed with reason; therefore, we are able to use our reason to understand the biological processes of fertility. Unlike a man, a woman is fertile only at certain times. God has built into the woman's body certain signs of fertility that can be discerned to tell her when she is fertile and when she is not. Likewise, since we are rational beings, we must submit our inclinations to rational guidance and not act on them simply from impulse.

There is another element of responsible parenthood, and this is one of the most crucial teachings in the whole encyclical. Many believe that the Catholic Church teaches that women are to have as many children as biologically possible. This is a myth. Regarding this, Paul VI wrote:

> With regard to physical, economic, psychological and social conditions, responsible parenthood is exercised by those who prudently and generously decide to have more children, and by those who, for serious reasons and with due respect to moral precepts, decide not to have additional children for either a certain or an indefinite period of time.[154]

The decision to raise a large family must be prudently and prayerfully arrived at by both husband and wife. The proper orientation to that discernment is generosity, as spouses are called to open their marriage to children. However, there may be times in a couple's marriage when the addition of a new life is not the responsible decision. In a case such as this, the choice must be made for serious reasons, with respect for the moral law, and in light of a well-formed conscience. It is important to keep in mind that marriage is not purely a relationship between a husband and wife. Marriage is a relationship that extends beyond the couple, to God, the family, and society. In order to exercise responsible parenthood authentically, spouses have a duty to consider these aspects when making their decisions.

The nature of marriage, conjugal love, and responsible parenthood are for the benefit of the spouses. The Church's teaching is meant to safeguard the sacredness and beauty of marriage and its mission in transmitting human life. The human person is called to the vocation of love, and that vocation demands a total gift of self. Anything less violates the inherent dignity of the human person and the call to love as expressed in the institution of marriage.

Prophetic Teaching

Paul VI articulated four consequences that would result if use of contraception became widespread in society: marital infidelity and a general lowering of morality; loss of respect for women; misuse of contraception by public authorities; and disregard of limits to man's dominion over his own body. He wrote:

> Let [us] first consider how easily this course of action could open wide the way for marital infidelity and a general lowering of moral standards. Not much experience is needed to be fully aware of human weakness and to understand that human beings — and especially the young, who are so exposed to temptation — need incentives to keep the moral law, and it is an evil thing to make it easy for them to break that law. Another effect that gives cause for alarm is that a man who grows accustomed to the use of contraceptive methods may forget the reverence due to a woman, and, disregarding her physical and emotional equilibrium, reduce her to being a mere instrument for the satisfaction of his own desires, no longer considering her as his partner whom he should surround with care and affection.
>
> Finally, careful consideration should be given to the danger of this power passing into the hands of those public authorities who care little for the pre-

cepts of the moral law. Who will blame a government which in its attempt to resolve the problems
affecting an entire country resorts to the same mea-
sures as are regarded as lawful by married people in
the solution of a particular family difficulty? Who
will prevent public authorities from favoring those
contraceptive methods which they consider more
effective? Should they regard this as necessary, they
may even impose their use on everyone. It could
well happen, therefore, that when people, either
individually or in family or social life, experience
the inherent difficulties of the divine law and are
determined to avoid them, they may give into the
hands of public authorities the power to intervene
in the most personal and intimate responsibility of
husband and wife.

Consequently, unless we are willing that the
responsibility of procreating life should be left to
the arbitrary decision of men, we must accept that
there are certain limits, beyond which it is wrong to
go, to the power of man over his own body and its
natural functions — limits, let it be said, which no
one, whether as a private individual or as a public
authority, can lawfully exceed.[155]

Sadly, the pope's warnings proved prophetic. Indeed, there
has been an increase in marital infidelity and a general lowering
of morality, as evidenced by the increasing numbers of divorces,
out-of-wedlock pregnancies, unmarried cohabitation, loss of the
child-centeredness of marriage, abortion, and the increase of sexually transmitted diseases. And this names just a few of the moral
issues facing us in our society today.

Who can deny that there has been a loss of respect for women?
Contraception provides men with the opportunity to engage in

the pleasures of conjugal love without a full, life-giving commitment. It allows men to use their wives for their own self-gratification. If a man pursues selfishness in the most intimate act with his wife, then it follows that selfishness will creep into other areas of his relationship with his wife.

Similarly, in many circumstances contraception has not only become a weapon in the hands of public authorities to dictate to their citizens the approved method of family planning, but it is also being used by government officials to deny the rights of citizens and religious organizations who disagree with contraception.

Furthermore, society insists there are no limits to the domination we have over our own bodies. Over the last fifty years, the human person's life-giving mission has been taken over by technology in ways that were unheard of when Paul VI wrote *Humanae Vitae*. Artificial insemination, in vitro fertilization, and embryonic-transfer techniques are now used as common means for couples to achieve pregnancy. We need only to look to the *Catechism* to see that every one of these techniques is immoral:

> Techniques involving only the married couple (homologous artificial insemination and fertilization) are perhaps less reprehensible, yet remain morally unacceptable. They dissociate the sexual act from the procreative act. The act which brings the child into existence is no longer an act by which two persons give themselves to one another, but one that "entrusts the life and identity of the embryo into the power of doctors and biologists and establishes the domination of technology over the origin and destiny of the human person. Such a relationship of domination is in itself contrary to the dignity and equality that must be common to parents and children."[156]

Paul VI has been called a weak and indecisive pope, but no one who lacked true courage could have issued the powerful statements he did or would have done so under the circumstances he faced.[157] Despite the obstacles he had to encounter along the way, the pope persevered and never gave up hope, even when he had more than enough reasons to be sad and despondent. Paul VI was simply a man of faith. "He did not have all the answers but he endured the suffering of all the questions. He worked for the good of humanity while trusting in the Lord. He once said, 'If only we can say Our Father and know what this means, then we would understand the Christian faith.'"[158]

Chapter Three Reflection Questions

Pope Saint John XXIII called the Second Vatican Council during a time of great turmoil because he knew that the Church had something to propose to the world, and he wanted to make sure the world could hear what the Church was offering. Specifically, what does the Church have to offer the world today?

The media shapes how we see the world. What do you do to verify that you have a clear understanding of the facts of any given situation?

From the 1960s until today, Catholics (clerical, religious, and lay) have felt free to debate openly the teachings of the Church. For example, with the release of every new papal document, there are people waiting in the wings to weigh in on whether they agree or disagree, and it goes on from there. Does this help or hurt the Church?

Pope Paul VI states that the problem of birth control cannot be considered without an understanding of the integral vision of man. How does such a comprehensive vision of the human person help us make choices that are in line with our dignity?

Has your perception of the Church's teaching on contraception changed over time? If so, in what way?

When properly used, modern methods of natural family planning are highly effective and pose no health risks for the women. Contraceptive devices such as the pill and the condom are proven to be less effective, and contraceptive medicines/devices can have side effects on a woman's health. Given this, why do couples overwhelmingly choose to use contraceptive devices?

CHAPTER FOUR

As the Family Goes, So Goes the World

John Paul II, *Familiaris Consortio*

FAMILY AND THE TRUE MEANING OF FREEDOM

Imagine, if you will, attending a meeting in Rome with over two hundred bishops from more than ninety countries, cultures, and languages, gathered together to discuss issues pertaining to the family in the modern world. This was the scene of Pope John Paul II's first synod of bishops,[159] held in Rome from September 26 to October 25, 1980. The topic of the synod was, "The Role of the Christian Family in the Modern World."

The meeting was nothing if not enlightening. It was an awesome experience of the universal Church discussing a variety of views pertaining to the family. Bishops from developing countries raised many issues dealing with such matters as family survival under difficult political and economic circumstances, the role of the state in determining family size, and the survival of the Christian family where Christians were a minority population. For industrialized countries, the concerns were more about internal family issues, such as contraception and the challenges of maintaining intimacy in marriage, the Church's response to divorce, the need for family spirituality, and the roles of women and men in the family. As one news article expressed the differences:

> Bishops from developing nations ... complained that the [preparatory] documents reflected first-world problems, not theirs. Bishops from India wanted to talk about interreligious marriages. And while first-world Catholics might have problems with birth control, the Indian bishops were fighting a government that wanted to impose limits on family size. Latin American bishops spoke of poverty as the root of marriage problems in their countries. Bishops from Africa spoke about polygamy.[160]

For nearly five weeks, the bishops deliberated on these matters and more. During those weeks, Pope John Paul II attended "virtually every general session, listening but never speaking and constantly taking notes. He invited each member of the Synod to lunch or dinner at the papal apartment, and he presided and preached at the opening and closing Masses."[161] At the end of the synod, the bishops were expected to come to a consensus regarding their deliberations and then submit their recommendations to the pope.

The 1980 synod discussions were not entirely collegial. According to papal biographer George Weigel, "the twelve years after *Humanae Vitae* had not produced agreement among the world's bishops on the crisis of family life in the modern world, or on the Church's marital ethic."[162] Some bishops thought they were being manipulated by Rome, while "others thought that those bishops pressing for a revision of the sexual ethic defended by *Humanae Vitae* had failed to grasp Paul VI's prophetic stance against the sexual revolution's assault on marriage."[163]

Still others thought that the discussions had paid little to no attention to the real problems of the modern family. Given that it is a controversial topic still today, it is interesting to note that the issue of the divorced and remarried receiving Communion was also discussed. And while John Paul II took all of these matters into consideration, he boiled it down to just one issue: the need for an adequate understanding of what it means to be human.

At the synod, the bishops called for the creation of theological centers devoted to studying the Church's teaching on marriage and the family. Pope John Paul II responded by establishing the Pontifical John Paul II Institute for Studies on Marriage and Family, as well as the Pontifical Council for the Family. Within a year, he also wrote the post-synodal apostolic exhortation[164] *Familiaris Consortio* (on the role of the Christian family in the modern world), which became one of his favorite teaching documents.

No pope in history has written and taught more on the topic of marriage and the family than Pope John Paul II, and *Familiaris Consortio* contains a rich and beautiful vision of a Christian family. And yet, "during his pontificate, the actual situation of marriage and family life deteriorated. The vision became more beautiful, but the reality more ugly."[165] During his twenty-seven-year pontificate, the world saw an increase in divorce, cohabitation, single parents, as well as the emergence of a worldwide homosexual culture.[166]

In spite of this, John Paul II held that the issues surrounding marriage and human sexuality were the bridge to the truth about love and about the human person. The truth is that we are created in the image of God, to be a communion of persons, and that man and woman are called to image Trinitarian love by being a total self-gift to one another. According to John Paul II, human beings are made "through love" and "for love," and because love is the fundamental and innate vocation of every human being, this vocation is the heart of marriage and the heart of the family.

In *Familiaris Consortio*, the pope connected the present-day problems regarding family life to what had already emerged as a key theme in his pontificate: the true meaning of freedom. The pope held that the issues of our day are rooted in distorted ideas of freedom, most particularly in the area of contraception. Agreeing with this premise, in an article commemorating the fiftieth anniversary of *Humanae Vitae*, author Mary Eberstadt writes:

> The promise of sex on demand, unencumbered by constraint, may be the strongest collective temptation humanity has ever encountered. That's why, since the invention of the birth control pill, resistance to the traditional Christian code has been unremittingly ferocious, and why so many in the laity and clergy wish that this rule — among others — were less taxing. As the disciples of Jesus Christ complained upon hearing his teaching about marriage, these lessons are "hard."[167]

Certainly, there are those who will forever consider the Church's teaching on contraception unreasonable. However, Pope John Paul II's presentation of the Church's understanding of contraception, which took a different angle from previous papal statements on the issue, did attract many people. Although he always maintained his defense of Pope Paul VI's *Humanae Vitae*, John Paul II framed the teaching in a new way.

Instead of stressing the procreative aspect of sexual intercourse and the wrongness of contraception in the eyes of God, which was the emphasis of *Humanae Vitae*, John Paul II emphasized the unitive end of marital intercourse and the harmful effect of contraception on this dimension of sexual love. In other words, he embraced the "yes!" of sexual love, and in doing so he painted a much more appealing picture, one that is open to life and all of its blessings. Franciscan University of Steubenville theology professor Dr. William Newton discusses this in his article entitled, "The Legacy of the Vision of Pope John Paul II for Marriage and Family." Newton claims that John Paul's main point was:

Contraception thwarts the total self-giving that should be part of marital intercourse. The idea is expressed in terms of ... the "language of the body" ... that the human body "speaks" in the conjugal act. It says: I am all yours (*totus tuus*). The problem with contraception, in light of this analysis, is that this very language is contradicted by the use of contraception. [In other words,] "the innate language that expresses the total reciprocal self-giving of husband and wife is overlaid, through contraception, by an objectively contradictory language, namely, that of not giving oneself totally to the other."[168]

The pope showed that contraception is a failure to make a sincere gift of oneself to one's spouse, which — since love and self-gift are synonymous — is a failure in love. So, contraception isn't just anti-life, it's anti-love. John Paul II wanted people to understand the profound difference between the pro- and the anti-contraceptive mentalities, for he well understood that "to support contraception and see it as normal behavior, or to oppose it, is to have two profoundly different views of what it means to be human."[169]

To him, marriage could never be simply a contract, nor could the family be simply a utilitarian convenience for its members.[170] He was unyielding in this conviction, believing that, "if even an inch of ground were given here, then the battle for the truth of the human person would be lost."[171] Actually, his teaching was always about much more than the family, it was about the whole concept of human life and love.

Unfortunately, the family situation today is more than a battle, it is an all-out war. Even in 1994, when John Paul II wrote his *Letter to Families*, he spoke to this reality: "[Today] the family is placed at the center of the great struggle between good and evil, between life and death, between love and all that is opposed to love."[172] He was certainly not alone in this belief.

In fact, just months before he died in September 2017, the late Cardinal Carlo Caffarra[173] spoke at a conference in Rome, telling the audience that the final battle over marriage and the family is being fulfilled in our own day.

"Satan is hurling at God this 'ultimate and terrible challenge,' to show he is capable of constructing an 'anti-creation' that mankind will be deceived into thinking is better than what God has created,"[174] Cardinal Caffarra warned. This conflict "is being fought in an interior and exterior dimension: within both the human heart and human culture."[175] A dire assessment, to be sure, but accurate nonetheless. This confrontation shows itself with "particular clarity"[176] in two developments, according to Caffarra. The first is "the transformation"[177] of the crime of abortion into a legal and subjective right; the second is equating a homosexual relationship to marriage.

One of the fundamental laws through which God governs the universe is that he does not act alone. In other words, every human person is "created" by God and "begotten" by its parents. The cardinal added, "marriage has a 'permanent structure' in the mind of God because the union of man and woman is the 'human cooperation in the creative act of God.'"[178]

Meanwhile:

> Legalized abortion "signifies calling what is good, evil, what is light, shadow." It is a Satanic attempt, to produce an "anti-Revelation," to generate an "anti-creation." By ennobling the killing of humans, Satan has "laid the foundations for his 'creation': to remove from creation the image of God, [and] to obscure His presence therein."
>
> The second development ... is the "ennoblement of homosexuality, which, in fact, denies entirely the truth of marriage in the mind of God, the Creator."[179]

When asked how the Church might better prepare for this current cultural crisis, the cardinal was completely candid:

> I believe — I'll say this right away — the point at which we have arrived is a station at the end of a long process. I am speaking of the West and a process that has lasted centuries. It would, therefore, be naive to think that in a few years — at times, I think, in a few generations — one could correct this process, turn it around. This must be said as a premise. It's not as if St. Benedict saw immediately the consequences of the communities he founded in the woods around Rome. It was necessary to have a whole process of civilization. We have to always remember this in order not to be naive.[180]

Cardinal Caffarra was well-positioned to speak with such authority on this topic, as the founding president of the Pontifical John Paul II Institute for Studies on Marriage and Family.[181] The Institute was founded for the purpose of studying the truth about the human person in all of its dimensions, with a particular emphasis on the person in relation to marriage and the family. For decades, Caffarra, a renowned scholar in moral theology and bioethics, was the Church's leading expert on the subject. He knew better than anyone that while the devil cannot attack God directly, he can make a mockery of the highest point of God's creation, the life-giving love between a husband and wife.

The cardinal frequently shared what it was like to prepare the Institute to begin its vital mission. As the story goes, he felt so overwhelmed by the intense spiritual battle that he was facing from both inside and outside of the Church, that he wrote to Sister Lúcia dos Santos,[182] the last survivor of the three Fátima visionaries, to request prayers. Even though they had never met in person, the cardinal had a special affection for her, as the Institute had been placed under the protection of Our Lady of Fátima.

To his surprise, he received a lengthy letter with her signature, now located in the archives of the Institute. At the end of this letter, Sister Lúcia did not mince words:

> The final battle between the Lord and the kingdom of Satan will be about Marriage and the Family. Don't be afraid, because whoever works for the sanctity of Marriage and the Family will always be fought against and opposed in every way, because this is the decisive issue.... *Nevertheless, our Lady has already crushed his head.*[183]

Indeed, Sister Lucia's words proved to be prophetic. On the day Pope John Paul was scheduled to announce the founding of the Pontifical John Paul II Institute for Studies on Marriage and Family, he was shot point-blank in the abdomen by a Turkish terrorist named Mehmet Ali Agca. It was May 13, 1981, the feast of Our Lady of Fátima. While this delayed the announcement, it did not delay the project. For not even the bullet from the barrel of an assassin's gun, in the midst of twenty thousand pilgrims and tourists gathered in Saint Peter's Square, could stop Pope John Paul II from emphasizing the issues of marriage and family. The Institute opened on October 7, 1982, the feast of Our Lady of the Rosary, and Cardinal Carlo Caffarra served as president until 1995.

Pope John Paul II believed that, in some mystical way, God had chosen him to suffer and that, in a particular way, he was to suffer for the sake of the family. He said as much in May 1994, shortly after returning to his apartment from a nearly monthlong stay in the hospital, recuperating from a broken hip. During the Sunday Angelus address, he said, "through Mary, I would like to express my gratitude today for this gift of suffering linked with this Marian month of May. I am grateful for this gift. I have understood that it is a necessary gift."[184] He continued:

I understand that I have to lead Christ's Church into this third millennium by prayer, by various programs, but I saw that this is not enough: she must be led by suffering, by the attack thirteen years ago and by this new sacrifice. Why now, why in this Year of the Family? Precisely because the family is threatened, the family is under attack. The Pope has to be attacked, the Pope has to suffer, so that every family may see that there is, I would say, a higher Gospel: the Gospel of suffering by which the future is prepared.[185]

Given the current state of the family, it might be tempting to wonder if the family today is struggling because Pope John Paul II's vision of marriage was somehow lacking. Is it possible that he did not do enough to help the family? Should he have started more programs? Written more? Suffered more? Hardly.

The family crisis that we are currently experiencing is not due to lack of Church teaching regarding marriage, divorce, homosexuality, and the like. No, the teaching is there for anyone who is willing to listen. Rather, it is a "crisis of confidence and a crisis of faith."[186] There is a lack of confidence in presenting the Church's teaching on marriage and family because many people (including many bishops and pastors) think the teaching is too demanding.

This crisis of faith, which has deeply affected the family, stems from our failure to remember that God has not left us to our own devices. Hidden in the Sacrament of Matrimony is an inexhaustible source of grace, a point that John Paul II makes abundantly clear in *Familiaris Consortio*. "With men this is impossible, but with God all things are possible" (Mt 19:26).

FAMILIARIS CONSORTIO

As a newly ordained priest, the future Pope John Paul II enjoyed the friendships of many young men and women who were just coming of age. He was simply drawn to them and would be for the rest of his life, something he recognized early in his priesthood. In fact, he once admitted, "I felt almost an inner call in this direction."[187]

All young people are drawn to love, and so he taught them to love. In fact, he once said that it was through these friendships that he "learned to love human love."[188] "Human love" became one of the fundamental themes of his entire priesthood. He spoke about it from the pulpit, in the confessional, and it is sprinkled throughout his writings. Again, in his article, "The Legacy of the Vision of Pope John Paul II for Marriage and Family," Dr. Newton explains:

> I have to say, that I find Wojtyla's[189] own understanding of human love, especially the love between a man and a woman, to be astoundingly profound. When one thinks about it, Wojtyla's exposure to happy family life and the dynamics of a husband and wife was very brief. His mother died when he was nine, his only sibling when he was 14, and his father when he was 21. But providence gave him a very acute insight into human love, including romantic love.[190]

Nevertheless, John Paul II possessed a realistic approach to the day in, day out realities of married love, which is reflected in *Familiaris Consortio*, a long document, divided into four main parts; it is written to all the faithful, and in a particular way to young people who are preparing for marriage and family life.

"Bright Spots and Shadows for the Family Today"

Part One, entitled "Bright Spots and Shadows for the Family Today," deals with the realities of our day, noting that there is an "interplay of light and darkness,"[191] both of which are influencing family life. It begins by taking up the subject of marriage in light of the Church's teaching, given the fact that contemporary culture poses many difficult challenges to the modern Christian.

The specific issues that will be addressed are outlined early in the document:

> The situation in which the family finds itself presents positive and negative aspects: the first are a sign of the salvation of Christ operating in the world; the second, a sign of the refusal that man gives to the love of God.
>
> On the one hand, in fact, there is a more lively awareness of personal freedom and greater attention to the quality of interpersonal relationships in marriage, to promoting the dignity of women, to responsible procreation, to the education of children. There is also an awareness of the need for the development of interfamily relationships, for reciprocal spiritual and material assistance, the rediscovery of the ecclesial mission proper to the family and its responsibility for the building of a more just society. On the other hand, however, signs are not lacking of a disturbing degradation of some fundamental values: a mistaken ... concept of the independence of the spouses in relation to each other; serious misconceptions regarding the relationship of authority between parents and children; the concrete difficulties that the family itself experiences in the transmission of values; the growing number of divorces; the scourge of abortion; the ever more frequent recourse to sterilization; the appearance of a truly contraceptive mentality....
>
> Worthy of our attention also is the fact that, in the countries of the so-called Third World, families often lack both the means necessary for survival,

such as food, work, housing and medicine, and the most elementary freedoms. In the richer countries, on the contrary, excessive prosperity and the consumer mentality, paradoxically joined to a certain anguish and uncertainty about the future, deprive married couples of the generosity and courage needed for raising up new human life: thus life is often perceived not as a blessing, but as a danger from which to defend oneself....

This shows that history is not simply a fixed progression towards what is better, but rather an event of freedom, and even a struggle between freedoms that are in mutual conflict, that is, according to the well-known expression of St. Augustine, a conflict between two loves: the love of God to the point of disregarding self, and the love of self to the point of disregarding God.[192]

It seems clear that Pope John Paul believed selfishness to be the root of the serious problems affecting family life today. Christian psychologist Paul Vitz calls today's "widespread and unrestrained self-interest (self-affirmation), the 'cult of self-worship.'"[193] Unfortunately, this mentality has led to a "growing fear, and even hatred, of new human life."[194]

The pope also denied the popular assumption that human history evolves at a fixed rate and always for the better. Instead, history has always been a struggle between two conflicting freedoms or loves. It is the age-old struggle between loving ourselves and loving God, compounded by all of the negative influences of the world today, to which Christians are not immune.

In fact, we live in an age in need of wisdom. "Our era needs such wisdom more than bygone ages if the discoveries made by man are to be further humanized. For the future of the world stands in peril unless wiser people are forthcoming."[195] Moreover, "the great task that has to be faced today for the renewal of society is that of recapturing the ultimate meaning of life and its fundamental values. Only an awareness of the primacy of these values enables man to use the immense possibilities given him by science in such a way as to bring about the true advancement of the human person in his or her whole truth, in his or her freedom and dignity. Science is called to ally itself with wisdom."[196]

"The Plan of God for Marriage and the Family"

Part Two, entitled "The Plan of God for Marriage and the Family," unpacks God's plan for marriage and family. A condensed version of Pope John Paul II's Theology of the Body, Part Two is the heart of this document. As with all of John Paul II's reflections on marriage, family, and human sexuality, the starting point is that God created us in his own image, out of love and for love, and that determines everything. "It raises the bar, so to speak, in all matters of human sexuality."[197]

We often take for granted the fact that we are made in God's image, yet it is an extraordinary statement about who we are and how we should act. Since God is love, and we are created in his image, we, too, are called to love. In fact, loving is our natural vocation. "Through Christian revelation, we know marriage is one way of living out that vocation, celibacy or virginity is the other."[198]

Our "personhood," which images God, is unique because it is enfleshed. Therefore, following the teaching of Pope John Paul II, our bodies express who we are as persons:

> Because our bodies express our persons, we cannot think of the body as something that simply "houses" the soul and, therefore, something which we can use, abuse, or alter as we see fit. What we do with our bodies, we do to ourselves. In a very real way, we *are* our bodies. And because our existence

is a total gift (that we had absolutely nothing to do with), we cannot say, in truth, that we "own" our bodies.

We are the only beings throughout creation who can manifest, bodily, how a person acts; we are the only beings who can reflect, in a physical way, what God *does*, that is, *love*. When we think of ourselves as made in God's image, we naturally and rightly think of our intellect and will — the thinking and deciding dimensions of our being. But, at the same time, we should realize that our bodies are a physical sign (sacrament) of our persons. We image God, therefore, with "mind and body."

As human persons, created male and female, we are called to express love in and through our bodies (Gn 2:18–24). One's sexual powers, then, are not only good but are a primary means of *loving* — giving oneself totally to another. How and in what context we express those powers reveals our very persons (since our bodies express our persons). Our sexuality and its expression, then, is virtually a window to our respective souls.[199]

By God's design, married love should be a *total* self-giving of each spouse to the other until death. Sexual intercourse, therefore, is meant to be the pinnacle of self-giving between man and woman. If a spouse withholds something, including the promise of future fidelity and commitment, then total self-giving does not exist in the relationship. The institution of marriage, with its promises of fidelity, commitment, and openness to life, is the only place where this total self-giving is possible.

Married love, by its very nature, does not stop with the unity between husband and wife, but naturally spills over into new life. Children are a living reflection of spousal love. And, for children, parental love is a concrete sign of God's love. Moreover, even when procreation is not possible, "conjugal life does not for this reason lose its value."[200] In fact, it "can be for spouses the occasion for other important services to the life of the human person, for example, adoption, various forms of educational work, and assistance to other families and to poor or handicapped children."[201]

It is important to realize that, in a Christian marriage, a child is born into two communities of love: the immediate family, and God's family, the Church. By way of the Christian family, the Church welcomes new generations, which, in turn, can enter the Church. Thus the family and the Church create a revolving door of mutual love and communion.

Part Two concludes with an important section on the mutually supportive vocations of virginity (celibacy) and marriage. Neither vocation would exist very well, if at all, without the other. Fidelity to the vocation of virginity or celibacy serves to strengthen fidelity within marriage.

"The Role of the Christian Family"

Part Three focuses on "The Role of the Christian Family." This section presents the four main tasks given to the Christian family in the modern world: building a communion of persons; serving life; participating in the development of society; and participating in the mission of the Church. For every married couple, the first task is to "become what you are."[202] This means that the family must become what it was originally designed to be, which is an "intimate community of life and love, whose mission is to guard, reveal, and communicate love."[203]

The perfect "communion of persons" is found in the Trinity, where each person gives himself totally to the other two. As human persons, we build a community of persons when we recognize the value in another (or others) and respond to that value by making a loving gift of ourselves. If another (or others) responds to us in kind, a true communion of persons comes into being. In the family, the husband and wife form a communion based on mutual self-giving love. Their love is the nucleus for a larger communion of persons including children, grandparents, and other members of the community.

That being said, this kind of love and communion is no easy task; it takes work. However, "without an ever-deepening communion of persons among family members, the Christian family cannot possibly fulfill its other major tasks of *serving life, helping develop society*, and *sharing in the life and mission of the Church*."[204] As if to reinforce this idea, Pope John Paul explains:

> Family communion can only be preserved and perfected through a great spirit of sacrifice. It requires, in fact, a ready and generous openness of each and all to understanding, to forbearance, to pardon, to reconciliation. There is no family that does not know how selfishness, discord, tension and conflict violently attack and at times mortally wound its own communion: hence there arise the many and varied forms of division in family life. But, at the same time, every family is called by the God of peace to have the joyous and renewing experience of "reconciliation," that is, communion reestablished, unity restored. In particular, participation in the sacrament of Reconciliation and in the banquet of the one Body of Christ offers to the Christian family the grace and the responsibility of overcoming every division and of moving towards the fullness of communion willed by God, responding in this way to the ardent desire of the Lord: "that they may be one."[205]

Up until now, the document has concentrated on the meaning

of an authentic communion of persons. Now we turn our attention to how that applies to individual members of the family, beginning with the roles and rights of women.

In summary, God created men and women with *equal* dignity and responsibility. Women have the right to pursue jobs in the public sector as long as it does not replace their maternal role in the home, and any form of degrading discrimination against women attacks the dignity of both men and women, blocking the possibility of a true communion of persons.

As for the responsibilities of the father in a communion of persons: the father must first respect the dignity of his wife and her role in the home. He must also recognize the importance of his role as nurturer and educator, as well as his responsibility for the "harmonious and united development of all the members of the family."[206] It is hard to overestimate the importance of the husband and father, particularly in our day and age.

With regards to other members of the family: "Special attention must be devoted to the children by developing a profound esteem for their personal dignity, and a great respect and generous concern for their rights. This is true for every child, but it becomes all the more urgent the smaller the child is and the more it is in need of everything, when it is sick, suffering, or handicapped."[207]

Regarding the elderly:

> There are cultures which manifest a unique veneration and great love for the elderly: far from being outcasts from the family or merely tolerated as a useless burden, they continue to be present and to take an active and responsible part in family life, though having to respect the autonomy of the new family; above all they carry out the important mission of being a witness to the past and a source of wisdom for the young and for the future.
>
> Other cultures, however, especially in the wake

of disordered industrial and urban development, have both in the past and in the present set the elderly aside in unacceptable ways. This causes acute suffering to them and spiritually impoverishes many families.

The elderly often have the charism to bridge generation gaps before they are made: how many children have found understanding and love in the eyes and words and caresses of the aging! And how many old people have willingly subscribed to the inspired word that the "crown of the aged is their children's children" (Prv 17:6)![208]

At this point in the exhortation, the focus shifts from building a community of persons to serving life, which, according to John Paul II, is the second task given to the Christian family. Here, it is important that parents willingly cooperate with God in the "transmission of life,"[209] something we have already discussed. It is also necessary for parents to educate their children toward the love and service of life, especially in the area of sex education:

Education in love as self-giving is also the indispensable premise for parents called to give their children a clear and delicate sex education. Faced with a culture that largely reduces human sexuality to the level of something common place, since it interprets and lives it in a reductive and impoverished way by linking it solely with the body and with selfish pleasure, the educational service of parents must aim firmly at a training in the area of sex that is truly and fully personal: for sexuality is an enrichment of the whole person — body, emotions and soul — and it manifests its inmost meaning in leading the person to the gift of self in love....

In this context education for chastity is absolutely essential, for it is a virtue that develops a person's
authentic maturity and makes him or her capable
of respecting and fostering the "nuptial meaning"
of the body. Indeed, Christian parents, discerning
the signs of God's call, will devote special attention
and care to education in virginity or celibacy as the
supreme form of that self-giving that constitutes the
very meaning of human sexuality.[210]

The Christian family's third major task is to "participate in the
development of society." In this regard, families are encouraged to
be socially and politically active. Just as the love between husband
and wife is meant to spill over into procreation and education of
children, the love within a family is meant to extend beyond its
own borders. At the same time, the family-society relationship is
not meant to be a one-way street. The state must protect and support the family in its own right and encourage family initiatives.
The moment the state tries to take over functions which are better
handled by families — sex education — it has overstepped its
bounds.

Finally, the fourth and last major task of a Christian family is
to share in the life and mission of the Church. Although there are
many ways to do this, we all are called to spread the good news of
the Catholic faith, particularly as it pertains to the Church's teaching on marriage and the family.

"Pastoral Care of the Family: Stages, Structures, Agents and Situations"

Part Four, "Pastoral Care of the Family: Stages, Structures, Agents
and Situations," discusses the need for the Church to become ever
more involved in supporting the family in all stages of life. The
Christian family has a major role in bringing Christ to the world,
and Pope John Paul II maintained that the Church must do ev-

erything in her power to support that, because the "future of the world and of the Church passes through the family."[211]

John Paul maintains that the family is where we get our first and most important glimpse of the character and quality of God's love, assuming, of course, that there is not significant conflict or even violence there. Is it any wonder, then, that while the Church is desperately trying to save the family, through education, healing, and love, that Satan is trying equally as hard to destroy it?

Chapter Four Reflection Questions

Consider whether the plight of the family would improve if the Church changed its teachings on marriage and family to allow for divorce, contraception, abortion, and homosexual unions.

Many doubt whether the average Catholic — let alone the average human being — is even capable of living the type of virtue that the Church teaches (in all situations). What do you think?

How does contraception change a couple's perspective on the world — not just on contraception, but on the human person and human love in general?

How would you respond to an engaged couple who said they were never going to bring children into a world that is constantly threatened with destruction? Or to someone who said that one-child families are our only hope for survival?

In your own mind, how is the future of the Church tied with the future of the family?

CHAPTER FIVE

Life Is Beautiful

John Paul II, *Evangelium Vitae*

FACING OUR CULTURE

As the crowd stood in Saint Peter's Square anxiously waiting to meet their new pope, the newly elected Pope John Paul II, sensing the drama and tension of the moment, brushed by his brother cardinals to get to the microphone on the loggia. He then introduced himself in Italian, their native language, and the people loved it:

> Dear Brothers and Sisters.... We are all still grieved after the death of our most beloved John Paul I. And now the eminent cardinals have called a new bishop of Rome. They have called him from a far country: far, but always near through the communion of faith and in the Christian tradition.[212]

Truly, on that Monday evening, October 16, 1978, the new pope's beloved Poland must have seemed very, very far away — far in distance, but always close to his heart. They say that to understand Pope John Paul II, the first non-Italian pope elected in 456 years, it is crucial to grasp and comprehend his Polishness, as it is the essential trait of his personality. To the end, John Paul (Karol Wojtyla) was a Polish nationalist, a Polish philosopher, a Polish poet, and a Polish politician. At Christmas, he ate Polish food prepared in a Polish way, sang Polish carols, and visited with his Polish friends.

By way of background, the thousand-year history of Poland has fashioned a profound separation between the Polish nation and the Polish state. The "nation," its language and cultural heritage, is rich in all of life's most important things. "Ever since Prince Mieszko, the medieval leader who united various Slavic tribes into a unified people, converted to Catholicism in 966, a Polish-speaking people have inhabited central Europe. Those people, who spread throughout the fields of central Europe, formed their own culture."[213] One might say that the nation of Poland is Polish to the bone.

The "state" of Poland has a much more complicated history. After a golden era of prosperity from the fourteenth to the sixteenth centuries, Poland was partitioned three times in the eighteenth century. By 1795, the state of Poland disappeared until the end of World War I in 1918. The Polish nation, its culture, literature, faith, and heritage, survived this period, not through governmental strength, but through the people drawing on their own cultural resources.[214]

The Polish habit of distinguishing between nation and state came easily to Karol Wojtyla. From his birth in 1920 until his sophomore year at the Jagiellonian University in Kraków, he lived in a Polish nation governed by a Polish state. However, that ended on September 1, 1939, "with the Nazi invasion of Poland from the West. When the Soviets invaded from the East seventeen days later, Poland endured another period of seeking to maintain itself as a nation without a state."[215]

Consequently, as a young man, Wojtyla devoted himself to the cultural life of literature, drama, and the theater under a totalitarian regime, and then studied for the priesthood in an underground seminary. He became a pastor and then a university professor before his appointment as bishop.

Under very difficult circumstances, Poland had maintained a healthy culture, because deep in their hearts the Polish people remained Polish. The Catholic Church had helped preserve this over the centuries through the protection of both language and culture. The late pope defined culture simply "as the specific way of human existence."[216] We can also understand it as a "shared way of life." As he explained it:

> The human person "is understood in a more complete way when he is situated within the sphere of culture through his language, history, and the position he takes towards the fundamental events of life, such as birth, love, work, and death. At the heart of every culture lies the attitude man takes to the greatest mystery: the mystery of God. Different cultures are basically different ways of facing the question of the meaning of personal existence."[217]

John Paul was deeply formed in his Catholic culture, and through this, he came to understand how culture intersects with human life. He once testified that Poland "has kept its identity, and it has kept, in spite of partitions and foreign occupations, its national sovereignty, not by relying on the resources of physical power, but solely by relying on its culture. This culture turned out in the circumstances to be more powerful than all other forces."[218]

Similarly, papal biographer George Weigel has argued that the Slavic view of history, which is centered on the role of culture, provides the true understanding of what moves peoples and societies at the deepest level. He writes:

> In this way of thinking, history is not simply the by-product of the context for power in the world....

Rather, history is driven, over the long haul, by culture — by what men and women honor, cherish, and worship; by what societies deem to be true and good and noble; by the expression they give to those convictions in language, literature, and the arts; by what individuals are willing to stake their lives on.[219]

Perhaps because he had been so steeped in this view of culture, John Paul II was painfully aware of the deep sickness in much of the culture across the world. While constantly emphasizing the need for a healthy and free culture, he warned that we are surrounded by and participate in a very different climate, a "culture of death"[220] and even an "anti-culture."[221] In a paper entitled, "What is the legacy of Pope John Paul II?," Professor Gregory R. Beabout vividly describes what this means:

A culture of death is an idea of society excessively concerned with efficiency. When efficiency becomes a primary good, those who are weak and vulnerable come to be viewed as useless, or as an intolerable burden. The result is a conspiracy against life. In this way, the pope analyzed our contemporary situation with regard to social and moral issues in cultural terms. The main problem isn't that we have bad laws. Rather, we face a distortion of the spirit. What is needed is a change of heart. Hence, the Pope's message calls us to promote a culture of life.[222]

John Paul II frequently referenced a quote by Pope Paul VI, saying that "the rupture between the Gospel and culture is 'without a doubt the drama of our time.'"[223] John Paul felt so strongly about culture that he went so far as to affirm, "Yes, the future of man depends on the culture."[224] Indeed, the crisis of faith in the world today largely stems from a crisis of culture, from a way of life that is opposed to the Gospel and draws Christians away from practicing their faith.

Turning away from God and focusing instead on the human has not led to liberation of culture, but rather to the devaluing of human life. Culture is meant to promote human flourishing, but today it has become an obstacle to a fulfilled human life, consistently threatening the moral being of the person, which is in many ways more serious than the physical attacks on life. The fight for Christian culture has become a fight for life itself.

We can be sure that Pope John Paul II was thinking and praying about all these things before he and the College of Cardinals held a three-day meeting in April 1991 to discuss the current threats to human life. The theme of the meeting was, "The Church facing the threat against human life and the challenge of the sects."[225]

As the meeting progressed, Cardinal Joseph Ratzinger zeroed in on moral relativism as the heart of the problem, particularly in the West. He knew that once moral relativism became legal in the name of tolerance, all basic human rights (such as the right to life) would be compromised, and the door would be open to totalitarianism. Ratzinger knew from his personal experience in Germany that a society that no longer knows how to make public arguments for absolute values cannot protect itself from evils such as Nazism. He stressed that abortion, euthanasia, and the manipulation of life for eugenic or experimental scientific ends are not "Catholic" issues — they are civilization issues.

The cardinals agreed that a cultural turning point had been reached. They "adopted a closing declaration that asked the Pope 'to give an authoritative voice and expression ... to the Church's Magisterium in regard to the dignity of human life.'"[226] It was, in effect, an invitation to write an encyclical. John Paul accepted.

The drafting process began with the pope writing a letter to every bishop in the world, asking their suggestions for the forthcoming document. He also received counsel from others with long public experience in pro-life activism. More than four years of consultation resulted in a 48,000-word encyclical, *Evangelium Vitae* ("The Gospel of Life"). It was the eleventh encyclical of John Paul's pontificate.

This letter was the pope's wake-up call for the West, which was (and still is) in danger of forgetting the painful lessons of the twentieth century, especially the brutal legacy of atheist, materialist ideologies that established death camps and gulags. "His suggestion that the West was also vulnerable to this death-dealing was regarded as an exaggeration by some when *Evangelium Vitae* was issued; no sane person denies the late pope's insight today."[227]

This encyclical presents the rise of legal abortion as a symptom of moral confusion. People are losing the ability to distinguish between good and evil in modern life. Far too many people in our culture "value life only to the extent that it brings pleasure and well-being,"[228] while "suffering seems like an unbearable setback, something from which one must be freed at all costs."[229] This inability to accept the reality of human suffering and the need to accompany those in distress is "one of the more alarming symptoms of the 'culture of death' ... marked by an attitude of excessive preoccupation with efficiency and which sees the growing number of elderly and disabled people as intolerable and too burdensome."[230]

In this document, John Paul II was pleading with the world to retrieve the spiritual and moral importance of an authentic culture. For, "lying deep in every culture there is an impulse toward fulfillment, goodness, truth, and life."[231] In *Evangelium Vitae*, he laid out one of the clearest expressions of how to build a new culture: we must promote a culture that defends and welcomes every human person.

EVANGELIUM VITAE

It is not every day that *Newsweek*, one of the leading U.S. news weeklies over the years, devotes a cover story to a papal encyclical. In fact, given the cultural climate of today, that seems nearly impossible. Nevertheless, that is exactly what happened in April 1995. Just days after the release of *Evangelium Vitae* on March 25, 1995, *Newsweek* ran a cover story entitled, "Life, Death, and the Pope." Religion editor Kenneth Woodward praised the letter as the clearest, most impassioned, and most commanding encyclical of the pontificate, one that would be John Paul's "signature statement" in history.[232]

Not only did the document appear in bookstores (which is not so unusual), it even appeared on supermarket checkout counters. "Evidently [it] spoke to a widespread concern that the use of abortion for 'family planning' and campaigns in favor of euthanasia bespoke a general coarsening, even cheapening, of life that ought to be resisted somehow."[233] In a mixed-up world such as ours, people were looking for clarity, and John Paul delivered.

Evangelium Vitae is a high-octane document that offers a robust framework for the renewal of Catholic moral teaching and the Church's engagement with mainstream culture. To this end, John Paul's language is unsparing. He calls democracies that deny the inalienable right to life from conception to natural death tyrant states[234] that betray the "long historical process ... that once led to discovering the idea of 'human rights.'"[235]

The encyclical, which consists of four lengthy chapters, addresses that age-old question: What is the meaning of life? Within that all-encompassing topic, the document speaks to some of the great mysteries of the human condition, including: What is truth? What is happiness? What is the purpose of suffering?

"The Voice of Your Brother's Blood Cries to Me from the Ground"

Chapter I, entitled "The Voice of Your Brother's Blood Cries to Me from the Ground," outlines the situation of the Western world in 1995, where assaults against human life led the pope to characterize the society as a "culture of death." Once again, the pope urged the Church to look back to the beginning, to the Book of Genesis, drawing heavily from the account of Cain and Abel, which shows how personal sin undermines the very basis for affirming love and life.

Cain was a farmer and his brother Abel was a shepherd. When it was time to offer sacrifices to God, Cain brought fruits from the ground (almost as an afterthought), while Abel brought the best, the fat portions from some of the firstborn of his flock. God favored Abel's sacrifice, but he did not extend that same grace to Cain. The rejection angered Cain, which led to God's admonishment, warning him that he was about to be consumed by sin.

Cain disregarded this warning, and instead took out his anger on his brother, killing Abel in a premeditated manner. Then God asked Cain where Abel was. Cain (now a child of sin and of the devil) lied and countered the all-knowing God with the infamous question, "Am I my brother's keeper?" The Lord's reply: "What have you done? The voice of your brother's blood is crying to me from the ground" (Gn 4:10).

God punished Cain for his sin: his efforts would no longer bear fruit and he would have to spend the rest of his life as a wanderer; "uncertainty and restlessness will follow him forever."[236] Upon hearing this, Cain cried to the Lord, "My punishment is greater than I can bear ... and whoever finds me will slay me" (Gn 4:13–14). After that, the Lord God, being full of mercy and grace, put a mark on Cain to keep him from being killed.

This story provides a framework within which we can more fully understand our relationship with God and our obligations to one another:

> The Lord's question: "What have you done?", which
> Cain cannot escape, is addressed also to the people
> of today, to make them realize the extent and gravi-
> ty of the attacks against life which continue to mark

human history; to make them discover what causes these attacks and feeds them; and to make them ponder seriously the consequences which derive from these attacks for the existence of individuals and peoples.[237]

Using the Genesis narrative, *Evangelium Vitae* draws out four important points. First, it shows that death did not come from God, but is the result of Satan's envy. We also see that man is not predestined to evil; rather, through his own free will, man chooses evil. Cain's sin was against the obligations of human solidarity, so the third point is that, yes, we are indeed our brother's keeper. Finally, in spite of sinful behavior, not even a murderer loses his dignity. God never stopped loving Cain.

From the story of Cain and Abel, through the prophets and the psalms, the Old Testament is a testimony to God's gift of life, demonstrating time and again that the killing of the innocent is a denial of that gift. This testimony is further expressed throughout the teachings and the life of Jesus Christ.

John Paul's platform for this encyclical as it pertains to the contemporary attacks on human life was as follows:

Some threats come from nature itself, but they are made worse by the culpable indifference and negligence of those who could in some cases remedy them. Others are the result of situations of violence, hatred, and conflicting interests, which lead people to attack others through murder, war, slaughter, and genocide.

And how can we fail to consider the violence against life done to millions of human beings, especially children, who are forced into poverty, malnutrition, and hunger because of an unjust distribution of resources between peoples and between social classes? And what of the violence inherent not only in wars as such but in the scandalous arms trade, which spawns the many armed conflicts, which stain our world with blood? What of the spreading of death caused by reckless tampering with the world's ecological balance, by the criminal spread of drugs, or by the promotion of certain kinds of sexual activity which, besides being morally unacceptable, also involve grave risks to life? It is impossible to catalogue completely the vast array of threats to human life, so many are the forms, whether explicit or hidden, in which they appear today!

[What about] another category of attacks, affecting life in its earliest and in its final stages, attacks which present new characteristics with respect to the past and which raise questions of extraordinary seriousness. It is not only that in generalized opinion these attacks tend no longer to be considered as "crimes"; paradoxically they assume the nature of "rights," to the point that the State is called upon to give them legal recognition and to make them available through the free services of health-care personnel. Such attacks strike human life at the time of its greatest frailty, when it lacks any means of self-defense. Even more serious is the fact that, most often, those attacks are carried out in the very heart of and with the complicity of the family — the family, which by its nature is called to be the "sanctuary of life."[238]

These attacks — and many others listed in the document — come from a distorted and perverse idea of "freedom." This idea, which is used to justify crimes against life under the umbrella of individual "rights," underlies the present conflict between the "culture of life" and the "culture of death."

How did we get here? The answer is not just cultural, but deeply personal as well:

> How did such a situation come about? Many different factors have to be taken into account. In the background, there is the profound crisis of culture, which generates skepticism in relation to the very foundations of knowledge and ethics, and which makes it increasingly difficult to grasp clearly the meaning of what man is, the meaning of his rights and his duties. Then there are all kinds of existential and interpersonal difficulties, made worse by the complexity of a society in which individuals, couples and families are often left alone with their problems. There are situations of acute poverty, anxiety or frustration in which the struggle to make ends meet, the presence of unbearable pain, or instances of violence, especially against women, make the choice to defend and promote life so demanding as sometimes to reach the point of heroism.[239]

"I Came That They May Have Life"

Chapter II is presented in the form of a meditation on the Christian understanding of life. It reviews the history of man created in the image and likeness of God, and then dives into the implications of this. Human life has its meaning within this context, and it is fulfilled only when it is in union with God. Yet sin darkens life by threatening it with death and throwing into doubt its nature as a gift. However, we are redeemed through the Incarnation, and the passion, death, and resurrection of Jesus Christ. The transcendent dignity of human life shines forth not only in the light of its origin, but even more so in the light of its destiny.

It is our responsibility to proclaim the "Gospel of Life," which includes not only the care for the innocent, weak, and vulnerable, but also by loving our enemies. Our moral responsibility for creation includes the environment, the natural world, and it involves participation in the creation of new life "in the image of God" as well.

Man is not the master of his life, nor is he the master of his death. Instead, man must always entrust himself to God, who has given him life. Because of this, "life is always a good. This is an instinctive perception and a fact of experience, and man is called to grasp the profound reason why this is so."[240] Consequently, suicide and euthanasia are always fundamentally immoral:

> Why is life a good? This question is found everywhere in the Bible and from the very first pages it receives a powerful and amazing answer. The life, which God gives man is quite different from the life of all other living creatures, inasmuch as man, although formed from the dust of the earth (cf. Gn 2:7, 3:19; Jb 34:15; Ps 103:14; 104:29), is a manifestation of God in the world, a sign of his presence, a trace of his glory (cf. Gn 1:26–27; Ps 8:6).[241]

Earthly life opens up to the prospect of eternal life. As good as it is, earthly life is not an absolute gift in itself. God entrusted man with life in order to be fruitful, and his life will reach its fullness if it succeeds in becoming a gift of love to God and to others. In other words, the gift of life is accomplished in self-giving. "No one, however, can arbitrarily choose whether to live or die; the absolute master of such a decision is the Creator alone, in whom 'we live and move and have our being.'"[242]

This chapter closes with a reflection on the mystery of suffering, because "more than anything else, it is the problem of suffering which challenges faith and puts it to the test."[243] To understand the mystery of suffering, each of us must look at "'the spectacle' of the Cross."[244] For the "Cross is not overcome by darkness; rather, it shines forth ever more radiantly and brightly, and is revealed as the center ... of all history and of every human life."[245] The paradox of life is that it finds its meaning when it is given up. In other words, the Gospel of Life is fulfilled on the Cross.

"You Shall Not Kill"

Chapter III is specifically devoted to the serious issues of abortion and capital punishment. The pope begins this chapter by examining the parable of the rich young man from the Gospel of Matthew:

> "And behold, one came up to him, saying, 'Teacher, what good deed must I do, to have eternal life?'" (Mt 19:16). Jesus replied, "If you would enter life, keep the commandments" (Mt 19:17). The Teacher is speaking about eternal life, that is, a sharing in the life of God himself. This life is attained through the observance of the Lord's commandments, including the commandment "You shall not kill." This is the first precept from the Decalogue which Jesus quotes to the young man who asks him what commandments he should observe: "Jesus said, 'You shall not kill, You shall not commit adultery, You shall not steal ... '" (Mt 19:18).
>
> God's commandment is never detached from his love: it is always a gift meant for man's growth and joy.... The Gospel of life is both a great gift of God and an exacting task for humanity.... In giving life to man, God demands that he love, respect and promote life.[246]

Each person is accountable and responsible for protecting and defending all human life. This includes not just the crime of abortion, but also any crime that involves the premeditated act of taking another person's life:

> The deliberate decision to deprive an innocent human being of his life is always morally evil and can never be licit either as an end in itself or as a means to a good end. It is in fact a grave act of disobedience to the moral law, and indeed to God himself, the author and guarantor of that law; it contradicts the fundamental virtues of justice and charity. "Nothing and no one can in any way permit the killing of an innocent human being, whether a fetus or an embryo, an infant or an adult, an old person, or one suffering from an incurable disease, or a person who is dying. Furthermore, no one is permitted to ask for this act of killing, either for himself or herself or for another person entrusted to his or her care, nor can he or she consent to it, either explicitly or implicitly. Nor can any authority legitimately recommend or permit such an action."
>
> As far as the right to life is concerned, every innocent human being is absolutely equal to all others.[247]

Moreover, "Whoever attacks human life, in some way attacks God himself."[248] And to those who argue that an embryo is not yet human life: "It would never be made human if it were not human already."[249] For this reason:

> It is true that the decision to have an abortion is often tragic and painful for the mother, insofar as the decision to rid herself of the fruit of conception is not made for purely selfish reasons or out of convenience, but out of a desire to protect cer-

tain important values such as her own health or a decent standard of living for the other members of the family. Sometimes it is feared that the child to be born would live in such conditions that it would be better if the birth did not take place. Nevertheless, these reasons and others like them, however serious and tragic, can never justify the deliberate killing of an innocent human being.[250]

Thus the pope writes: "Therefore, by the authority which Christ conferred upon Peter and his successors.... *I declare that direct abortion, that is, abortion willed as an end or as a means, always constitutes a grave moral disorder,* since it is the deliberate killing of an innocent human being."[251]

For anyone who has ever had an abortion or been involved with one, these must seem like very harsh words. However, our God is merciful, and his firmness is matched only by his tenderness. Pope John Paul II expressed this mercy of God beautifully, speaking to women who have had an abortion:

> I would now like to say a special word to women who have had an abortion. The Church is aware of the many factors which may have influenced your decision, and she does not doubt that in many cases it was a painful and even shattering decision. The wound in your heart may not yet have healed. Certainly what happened was and remains terribly wrong. But do not give in to discouragement and do not lose hope. Try rather to understand what happened and face it honestly. If you have not already done so, give yourselves over with humility and trust to repentance. The Father of mercies is ready to give you his forgiveness and his peace in the Sacrament of Reconciliation. To the same Father

and his mercy you can with sure hope entrust your
child. With the friendly and expert help and advice
of other people, and as a result of your own painful
experience, you can be among the most eloquent
defenders of everyone's right to life. Through your
commitment to life, whether by accepting the birth
of other children or by welcoming and caring for
those most in need of someone to be close to them,
you will become promoters of a new way of looking
at human life.[252]

The pope also addressed capital punishment, declaring that the
justification for the death penalty is "very rare, if not practical-
ly nonexistent."[253] Previously, the Church had always taught that
the punishment must be proportionate to the crime, and that the
death penalty must necessarily be reserved for grave matters. But
Evangelium Vitae stressed an additional condition: the death penalty must be reserved for cases of "absolute necessity,"[254] meaning
"when it would not be possible otherwise to defend society."[255]
While this may seem like a small matter, it was big enough that
the *Catechism of the Catholic Church* was changed to reflect this
nuance.

"You Did It to Me"

The concluding chapter of this landmark encyclical is an official
Catholic call to arms. As Catholics, we are a people of life, and as
such we are summoned to build a new "culture of life." "We have
been sent as a people. Everyone has an obligation to be at the
service of life".[256]

To be truly a people at the service of life we must
propose these truths constantly and courageous-

ly from the very first proclamation of the Gospel, and thereafter in catechesis, in the various forms of preaching, in personal dialogue and in all educational activity. Teachers, catechists, and theologians have the task of emphasizing the anthropological reasons upon which respect for every human life is based. In this way, by making the newness of the Gospel of life shine forth, we can also help everyone discover in the light of reason and of personal experience how the Christian message fully reveals what man is and the meaning of his being and existence. We shall find important points of contact and dialogue also with nonbelievers, in our common commitment to the establishment of a new culture of life.[257]

Beyond this list of professionals, there are "healthcare personnel: doctors, pharmacists, nurses, chaplains, men and women religious, administrators, and volunteers,"[258] whose "profession calls for them to be guardians and servants of human life."[259] In addition, intellectuals, particularly from Catholic universities, and from centers, institutes, and committees of bioethics, as well as politicians and civic leaders, and all people of goodwill are called to take part in building a culture of life:

The Gospel of life is for the whole of human society. To be actively pro-life is to contribute to the renewal of society through the promotion of the common good. It is impossible to further the common good without acknowledging and defending the right to life, upon which all the other inalienable rights of individuals are founded and from which they develop. A society lacks solid foundations when, on the one hand, it asserts values such as the dignity of the person, justice and peace, but then, on the other hand, radically acts to the contrary by allowing or tolerating a variety of ways in which human life is devalued and violated, especially where it is weak or marginalized. Only respect for life can be the foundation and guarantee of the most precious and essential goods of society, such as democracy and peace.[260]

Chapter Five Reflection Questions

Ponder the differences between the Polish nation and the Polish state. How was it possible for the Polish nation of Pope John Paul II's era to remain intact when the Polish state went through so many changes?

Consider the idea that the culture of death is a society excessively concerned with efficiency. What are the different ways that this presents itself in our everyday life?

The world at large is currently experiencing a crisis of faith. How is this connected to the cultural crisis of our day?

No sin is ever only individual. How do attacks against life affect every other person?

What was once recognized as evil is now seen as a social good in modern culture, as men and women drift away from God and demand the "freedom" to choose whatever they want. How do you explain this transformation in light of our current cultural crisis?

How are we, as a "people of life," to evangelize the world with the Gospel of Life, and who among us is called to do it?

CHAPTER SIX

Where Have All the Women Gone?

John Paul II, *Mulieris Dignitatem*

A NEW FEMINISM

Legend has it that Pope Saint John Paul II's mother, Emilia, would walk him in a baby carriage through his hometown of Wadowice, Poland, telling her neighbors, "You'll see, my Lolek will be a great man someday."[261] She was right. Unfortunately, she did not live long enough to see it. Just as he was finishing third grade, Emilia died of kidney failure and heart disease.[262]

After the death of his mother, the main influences in young Karol Wojtyla's education and spiritual formation were men, with his father, Karol, at the top of the list. In spite of this, there was always a special place in the heart of young Karol for women, particularly women who were mothers. Even though he was without his mother, numerous women surrounded him, often mothers and grandmothers of his friends, who felt it was their duty to help take care of him.

He recognized in them a "special something," an intuition of sorts, and, later in life, he gave that special intuition a name, calling it the "genius of woman"[263] or the "feminine genius."[264] As he grew older, he realized that "this intuition is linked to women's physical capacity to give life,"[265] and even if a woman never becomes a mother in the physical sense, this capacity has a profound effect on her personality.

During his papacy, John Paul II never shied away from promoting the traditional roles of women as mothers and homemakers. Perhaps his own experience convinced him of the importance of the homemaker, and it troubled him that some Western societies place such low value on this vastly important work. He admitted as much when talking about his apostolic letter[266] *Mulieris Dignitatem* (on the dignity and vocation of women) shortly after it was written:

> If our century has been characterized in liberal societies by a growing *feminism*, it might be said that this trend is *a reaction to the lack of respect accorded each woman*. Everything that I have written in *Mulieris Dignitatem* I have felt since I was very young, and, in a certain sense, from infancy. Perhaps I was also influenced by the climate of the time in which I was brought up — it was a time of great respect and consideration for women, especially women who were mothers.... [Sadly, in today's culture] woman has become, before all else, an object of pleasure.[267]

Never once did Pope John Paul II say that women should not work outside of the home, nor would he. Rather, he encouraged women to bring their "feminine genius" into the workplace and the world at large, where it is needed the most. In his 1995 *Letter to Women*, he wrote:

> Thank you, *women who work!* You are present and active in every area of life — social, economic, cul-

tural, artistic and political. In this way, you make an
indispensable contribution to the growth of a culture, which unites reason and feeling, to a model
of life ever open to the sense of "mystery," to the
establishment of economic and political structures
ever more worthy of humanity.[268]

As the late pope was coming of age as a young man, however, it
was difficult for him to ignore that the world at large was moving
toward something quite different from what he had known as a
child. He recognized that a radical, secular feminism was quickly
becoming one of the most troublesome cultural issues of the day.
Still prevalent today, this brand of feminism promotes a concept of
individual rights and personal autonomy which challenge the very
meaning of the feminine person.

Secular feminism began as a response to discrimination and
violence against women, but before long it became a movement
to liberate women from everything, including and especially their
bodies by controlling their fertility. In our own day this movement has further evolved into the issue of "gender equality," the
idea that men's and women's bodies are irrelevant, and even inter-
changeable.

John Paul II fully agreed that all discrimination and violence
against women is terribly wrong. Yet he held that "the liberation
of women from these patterns of domination can never be a liberation *against*. It must be a liberation *for*, one that safeguards the
distinctive vocation of women and men."[269]

Because this was and continues to be an area that needs the
light of the Christian perspective, Pope John Paul II was determined "to help women recover their dignity and to acknowledge
their specific role in society and the life the Church."[270] He held
that there were few areas more misunderstood than the Church's
teaching on women. In fact, in spite of significant criticism, John
Paul insisted that the Catholic Church has always been in defense

of the dignity of women and has offered a "consistent *protest* against whatever offends [that dignity.]"[271]

The 1987 Synod on the Laity provided just the opening he needed to correct these misunderstandings. This Synod of Bishops,[272] held in the tenth year of his pontificate, gathered in Rome to consider a much-discussed topic: "The Vocation and Mission of the Laity in the Church and in the World Twenty Years after the Second Vatican Council."

In preparation for this gathering, *Crisis* magazine published a number of articles written by various people, with each one entitled, "Preparing for the Synod on the Laity." All of these articles display the level of confusion regarding the role of laity, particularly among women, in a Church that was still adjusting to the directives of the Second Vatican Council. Perhaps author Charlotte Hays put it best:

> As a reporter, I've been fascinated by the bizarre spectacle of lay people clamoring to get on the altar while priests flee the sanctuary in droves. While lay people dispense Holy Communion, priests dispense political wisdom. We're definitely going through a topsy-turvy period. I only hope some contemporary comic genius is recording the havoc. But on a spiritual level, it isn't very funny. A stint on the women's ordination trail has shown me how much rancor results from confusion over one's vocation....
>
> Many Catholics, especially feminists, are veering towards a Protestant ideology of the priesthood of all believers. As so many Protestant churches have amply demonstrated, however, the priesthood of all believers inevitably degenerates into the priesthood of nobody, and finally into complete secularization; the world needs priestcraft.[273]

Catholic historian James Hitchcock gave a similar assessment:

> Lay and clerical roles have been redefined in a way
> that almost seems like a simple reversal: lay people
> press forward eagerly to discharge formal liturgical
> tasks previously reserved to clerics, while priests
> and religious aggressively crowd into what were
> previously considered lay professions, even ... re-
> nouncing their religious status in order to do so.
>
> Devout lay people seem to say that they cannot
> fully live their faith unless they perform recogniz-
> ably priestly tasks, even as priests complain of be-
> ing confined in the sanctuary. It may occur to the
> disinterested observer that such reversals betoken
> not so much deeper understanding or creative re-
> definition as simple confusion and formless discon-
> tent.[274]

Indeed, it was a confusing time, and we continue to experience
the effects of that confusion in the Church today. At the end of the
synod, John Paul's brother bishops asked him to develop "a further
study of the anthropological and theological bases that are needed
in order to solve the problems connected with the meaning and
dignity of being a woman and being a man."[275] In response to this
request, in August 1988 the pope published *Mulieris Dignitatem*,
which speaks to "the reason for and the consequences of the Creator's decision that the human being should always and only exist
as a woman or a man."[276]

Later that year, Pope John Paul II also published the promised
post-synodal exhortation[277] *Christifideles Laici* (on the vocation
and the mission of the lay faithful in the Church and in the world).
This document was the final word on the 1987 Synod of Bishops.
It included, among other things, "proposals of a pastoral nature on
the place of women in the Church and society."[278]

Toward the end of *Christifideles Laici*, the pope acknowledged, "If anyone has this task of advancing the dignity of women in the Church and society, it is women themselves, who must recognize their responsibility as leading characters."[279] With this, he builds upon the words from the Closing Message of the Second Vatican Council, which highlights that "the hour is coming" for women to realize their influence and their calling in the world. This message warns us that the human race is undergoing a frightening transformation, and that armed with the spirit of the Gospel women can and must help keep humanity from falling.[280]

From these teachings flowed John Paul II's distinctive brand of Christian feminism, a "new feminism." *Mulieris Dignitatem* provides both the theological and philosophical underpinnings for this new feminism. The pope later advanced these same ideas by putting them into public policy with his *Letter to Women,* which he wrote on the eve of the United Nations Fourth World Conference on Women, held in Beijing, China.

Former Vatican ambassador and Harvard law professor Mary Ann Glendon unpacks the significance of *Mulieris Dignitatem* and the *Letter to Women* with the following words:

> In a remarkable series of writings, [John Paul II] has meditated more deeply than any of his predecessors on the roles of women and men in light of the word of God. *Mulieris Dignitatem*, which contains the main theological basis for his messages to women, labels discrimination against women as sinful, and repeatedly emphasizes that there is no place in the Christian vision for oppression of women.
>
> The tone of all these writings to and about women is dialogical. Their author invites women to help him and the Church reflect upon the quest for equality, freedom, and dignity in the light of

faith — in the context of a changing society where the Church and the faithful are faced with new and complex challenges.[281]

Pope John Paul II's teaching on the dignity and vocation of woman as expressed in *Mulieris Dignitatem* was a new presentation directed to the current times. However, the truths themselves were not wholly new, as the pope highlighted in the opening paragraphs. It was common for him to look back at the same time he was pointing forward. In doing this, he showed the importance of stopping to evaluate and learn from the past before charting the future.

John Paul placed this apostolic letter in the context of the writings that preceded it. Setting it in the historical context of the Catholic Church's constant teaching serves as a reminder that Church doctrine is organic. This means that even though these teachings are intrinsic to the Faith, as the years pass they continue to be gradually, naturally, and prayerfully developed while adhering to the fundamental truths, so that they may be articulated to new generations and situations.

As we review *Mulieris Dignitatem*, it is important to understand that Pope John Paul II did not mean for it to be an academic or intellectual exercise. Rather, as he himself expressed it, "It seems to me that the best thing is to *give this text the style and character of a meditation.*"[282] A meditation requires that we take a truth and ponder it over and over again, reflecting on it from various perspectives, while asking the Holy Spirit to give us a clearer and deeper understanding of the text.

MULIERIS DIGNITATEM

Pope John Paul II once told the wife of the United States ambassador to the Vatican that her job as a wife and mother was much more difficult than his.[283] And he believed it, partly out of his admiration for the gift of motherhood, but also because he knew very well that the twentieth century had not been kind to women.

With each passing year, Pope Paul VI's predictions about women in *Humanae Vitae* seem more and more prophetic. Indeed, we have become a contraceptive society, and the general loss of respect for women is increasingly obvious. Just as Paul VI predicted, there has been an increase in marital infidelity and a general lowering of morality, divorce numbers have steadily increased, as have cohabitation and out-of-wedlock pregnancies, fatherless children, abortion, and sexually transmitted diseases.

A Sign of the Times

Seeing these social realities, Pope John Paul II, in *Mulieris Dignitatem*, considered the question, What is the mystery of woman? Who is this masterpiece of God's creation?

He began by acknowledging the many gifts that women have brought to the life of the Church, pointing to the teaching of the first two women Doctors of the Church, Saint Teresa of Avila and Saint Catherine of Siena. Echoing the words of Pope Paul VI, he wrote that "it is evident that women are meant to form part of the living and working structure of Christianity in so prominent a manner that perhaps not all their potentialities have yet been made clear."[284]

As was customary in his writing, Pope John Paul began *Mulieris Dignitatem* by looking back to "the beginning" of sacred Scripture to discover what makes woman different from man and the rest of creation, and what God originally intended.

It is interesting to note that the pope wrote this letter in 1988, during a Marian Year, a year specifically designated by the Church to increase our love and awareness of the Blessed Mother. The renewal of Marian theology and devotion was yet another characteristic of the papacy of Pope John Paul II. In fact, he dedicated his entire pontificate to Mary, as evidenced by the motto he chose for his papacy, *Totus Tuus*, which means, "I am entirely yours."

Not surprisingly, Mary is the common thread throughout John

Paul's meditation on the dignity and vocation of women. Because of her "yes" to the Angel Gabriel, and her cooperation with God's plan for redemption, salvation is possible for every one of us. For this reason, Mary is "the 'yes' of mankind to God's plan."[285] The reason that Mary is so important to the Catholic understanding of the world is because she was the first Christian, the perfect model of the Church, and the perfect model for each of us as individual disciples. Truly, "we are all called to be Mary."[286]

"Woman — Mother of God (Theotókos)"

The second chapter of *Mulieris Dignitatem*, dedicated to the Blessed Mother, is titled "Woman — Mother of God (Theotókos)." Theotókos means Mother of God. This tells us much about the Virgin Mary, but it also tells us a great deal about God. To begin with, it speaks of God's humility, for it makes clear that God wanted a mother! It also speaks of the reality that "it is through motherhood that humanity was given its Savior."[287]

God created us to be in union with him. Our hearts long for him, and, more importantly, he longs for us. In fact, so strong was this longing that "when the time had fully come, *God sent forth his son, born of woman*."[288] In this way, God fulfilled the mystery of our salvation, a mystery that he recognized and longed for from the beginning.

This event marked a turning point in human history, in that God personally united himself with the entire human race, elevating not only the dignity of the Blessed Mother, but also the dignity of every human being. Yet Mary alone gave birth to Our Lord, and she has a special place in this salvific event. Mary is the "woman" who marked the "fullness of time," and it is in her and through her that our salvation is realized.[289] When Mary gave her consent, her "fiat," she became "the handmaid of the Lord" (Lk 1:38).

We can safely say that the birth of Christ changed everything. It was the turning point of human history. In a very real way, one age ended and another began. By sending us his Son, God literally reached into human history and redeemed us from the predicament and consequence of the original sin of Adam and Eve.

The Annunciation and the Incarnation of Christ marked the beginning of this new age, and as *Mulieris Dignitatem* reminds us, "a woman is to be found *at the center of this salvific event.*"[290] "Mary is the first link between heaven and earth,"[291] and through the act of her obedience, God unites himself "in some fashion with every man."[292] What began with the Annunciation and Incarnation culminated in Christ's passion, death, and resurrection — the Paschal Mystery[293] — the event that redeemed mankind.

When the Virgin Mary gave birth to Christ, she brought to light the extraordinary dignity of the "woman." For example, in his Letter to the Galatians, Saint Paul writes, "born of woman" (Gal 4:4) instead of "born of Mary." Interestingly, this verse would have lost its significance if he had not referred to Mary this way. By saying "born of woman," Saint Paul implies that not only the dignity of Mary but the dignity of *every* woman is elevated.

The final section of Chapter II, "To serve means to reign," places us at the scene of the Annunciation, overhearing the conversation between the Angel Gabriel and the Blessed Mother. In this conversation, Mary demonstrates immense faith, which would be impossible without the grace of God. By calling herself "the handmaid of the Lord" Mary models for us the "dignity of service, the dignity which is joined in the closest possible way to the vocation of every person."[294] With this response, she takes her place within Christ's mission of service, advancing his kingdom in which "to serve ... means to reign."[295]

"The Image and Likeness of God"

Chapter III, "The Image and Likeness of God," turns again to the Book of Genesis, focusing on the climax of the entire creation story found in Genesis 1:27: "God created man in his own image, in the image of God he created him; male and female he created them." These words establish the fact that man and woman are equal, and together they are the image of God:

> This concise passage contains fundamental anthro-
> pological truths: man is the high point of the whole
> order of creation in the visible world; the human
> race, which takes its origin from the calling into ex-
> istence of man and woman, crowns the whole work
> of creation; both man and woman are human be-
> ings to an equal degree, both are created in God's
> image. This image and likeness of God, which is es-
> sential for the human being, is passed on by the man
> and woman, as spouses and parents, to their descen-
> dants: "Be fruitful and multiply, and fill the earth
> and subdue it" (Gn 1:28). The Creator entrusts do-
> minion over the earth to the human race, to all per-
> sons, to all men and women, who derive their dig-
> nity and vocation from the common "beginning."[296]

According to John Paul, this "revealed truth concerning man as
the 'image and likeness' of God constitutes the immutable basis
of all Christian anthropology."[297] In other words, if we want to
understand humanity, we must start from the fact that we are created not as generic human beings but as *male* and *female*, in God's
image. We derive our dignity and vocation from this common "beginning."[298]

Only "man is a person, man and woman equally so,"[299] meaning we are set apart, different from all other creatures. Scripture
verifies it is only after the creation of man (as male and female) that
God looked at all of his creation, "and behold, it was very good"
(Gn 1:31). Hence, from the beginning, we see that humanity is
articulated as male and female, and it is this "humanity, sexually
differentiated, which is explicitly declared 'the image of God.'"[300]

Our intellect tells us that we are different from the animals.
We understand that we are a "someone" and not a "something."

Similarly, our free will enables us to be the master of our choices, and only as human beings can we know the truth and act in accordance with it. This is not something the other animals are capable of. Therefore, human beings are the only creatures on earth "able to know and love [their] creator."[301]

It is only through loving that both men and women become fully human. We see this truth in man's first words, found in Genesis 2:23: "This at last is bone of my bones / and flesh of my flesh; / she shall be called Woman, / because she was taken out of Man." In his response, man recognizes that the woman shares his human nature, albeit embodied in a different way.

This passage from Genesis confirms in a definitive way the significance of the sexual differences between men and women. They are made for each other physically as well as ontologically, which is to say that they are made for union in the very essence of their being. This union is lived out through sexual expression, but also in spiritual, emotional, and psychological ways.

In *Mulieris Dignitatem*, John Paul II explains that we are to read the first two chapters of Genesis as one single narrative. The two creation accounts give us a profound understanding of what it means to be created in the image and likeness of God. The first narrative tells us that man and woman are created in God's image and likeness, and that each is a rational and free human being. The second account speaks to the truth that, while man and woman each have the dignity of personhood, this personhood is not to be lived out in radical individuality, but rather as a unity of the two in service to one another.

Within these creation accounts, "we find the heart of God's original plan and most especially and the deepest truth about man and woman."[302] The reality of living "for the other" is expressed in the "unity of the two,"[303] found in the covenant of marriage. However, this reality can also be fruitfully lived within the single life and the consecrated life, in which the beauty of spiritual fertility is richly expressed.

The whole truth about the mystery of the human person can be found in one of the sections in Chapter III: "Person — Communion — Gift." We know that man is not meant to be alone, that he is called to "exist only as a 'unity of the two,' and therefore *in relation to another human person.*"[304] To be human means to be a person, rational and free, created for relationship and created out of love for the purpose of love. It is for this purpose alone that we were created, which reveals something very important about God, our Creator, for the communion of love between persons is a reflection of the inner life of the Trinity.

However, marriage is by no means the only manifestation of the male/female relationship. The call to interpersonal communion is lived out in other ways, as is demonstrated in the commandment to "love one another" (Jn 13:34). In fact, the whole of human history unfolds within the context of this call to "communion."[305] In essence, "being a person means striving towards self-realization ... which can only be achieved '*through a sincere gift of self.*'"[306] The human ethos is to love one another as God loves us. And as we know, God's love knows no limits.

"Eve-Mary"

Chapter IV of **Mulieris Dignitatem** is aptly named "Eve-Mary," with the first section titled "The 'beginning' and the sin." This chapter delves deeper into the devastating effects of original sin described in Genesis 3. "Even though what is written in the Book of Genesis is expressed in the form of a symbolic narrative,"[307] it confirms an event that took place at the beginning of human history. This means that "we can only speculate, as did the *Genesis* writer,"[308] about the specifics of this first stage of life in the Garden of Eden. Nevertheless, through the "light of Revelation,"[309] we know that God tested our first parents and that they failed the test.

God gave our first parents the gift of freedom, so that they might draw closer to him, to each other, and to their destiny.[310] "God asked them — as he asks us — to recognize their human limits and to trust in him."[311] Adam and Even had everything imaginable, but the serpent's promise that "you will be like God" (Gn 3:5) was a temptation they simply could not resist. They chose themselves over God, and in doing so the splendor they had once enjoyed was now "miserably and thoroughly wrecked."[312]

So, while our first parents were free to make their choice, they were not "free to choose the consequences of their choice."[313] These consequences were disastrous, not only for them, but for the entire human race. In fact, it is impossible to understand what happened then, and what is still happening now, unless we clearly grasp the results of the fall of Adam and Eve. This is what John Paul II referred to in *Mulieris Dignitatem* as "'the mystery of sin,' and even more fully, 'the mystery of evil.'"[314]

By setting his own will against God's, Adam destroyed the love between himself and God, and as a result the supernatural life within him died. Consequently, all he had left was his natural life, but it bore little remembrance to what he had previously known. The faculties of his body and soul were no longer in harmony. There was a "disunity — not only between man and God but among human beings, between human beings and the created world, and even within the human being between spirit and body."[315] This disunity is the result of original sin.

Thus the burden of sin has grave consequences in any relationship, but most especially in a marriage, because marriage is a relationship that requires respect for and the realization of the dignity of each person. Because of the hereditary nature of sin, however, we are inclined to stray from what we know to be true and right. Our moral compass is askew and we are susceptible to sins described by Saint John as "the lust of the flesh and the lust of the eyes and the pride of life" (1 Jn 2:16), which plague the intimate marriage relationship in a significant way.

The original sin of Adam and Eve affected men and women differently. From generation to generation, women have tried to possess men and men have tried to dominate women. No matter how we play it out, it is sin, and sin is serious.

Sadly, today this tension between men and women, which leads to many injustices on both sides, is often boiled down to a deep-seated cultural bias against women. John Paul II explained that the question of "women's rights" has highlighted the problems between men and women, particularly in those circumstances where a woman is denied the same dignity as a man. In fact, this thinking has become the basis for the feminist rallying cry for equal rights, as evidenced in the MeToo movement that sprang up through social media beginning in late 2017.[316]

John Paul II agreed that women have not always been treated fairly. Yet the root of this domination is not cultural (although it is transmitted through culture), it is the result of sin. Sin has fractured the community of persons that God ordained from the beginning. As serious as this is, Pope John Paul II warned against any temptation that might lead to the "masculinization" of women. This is a frequent mistake made in the name of secular feminism.

The pope cautioned, "In the name of liberation from male 'domination,' women must not appropriate to themselves male characteristics contrary to their own feminine 'originality.'"[317] Rather, this deep cultural crisis of our time demands a clear and persuasive Christian response. All of us must reject "the temptation of imitating models of 'male domination,' in order to acknowledge and affirm the true genius of women in every aspect of the life of society, and overcome all discrimination, violence and exploitation."[318]

"Jesus Christ"

As we move on, we see that *Mulieris Dignitatem* is beautiful not only in its subject matter, but also in its design. Chapter V is appropriately titled "Jesus Christ." It is no accident that the precise center of this document's text highlights Our Lord, given that he is the center of our faith. In an effort to draw us into the mystery of Christ, the document invites us to explore a number of passages from the Gospels of Matthew, Mark, Luke, and John, all of which feature Jesus' interactions with women.

Considering the social norms of the first-century Jewish culture in which Jesus lived, his understanding of the roles of women was quite revolutionary. He embraced women as disciples and encouraged them to travel with him and participate in his ministry. In fact, not only did Jesus accept women as disciples, he also considered women equal to men as beneficiaries of God's blessing and in the responsibilities that come with God's grace.[319]

Clearly, when "Christ speaks to women about the things of God, they understand them; there is a true resonance of mind and heart, a response of faith."[320] Here John Paul II gives us a few examples of this:

> As we scan the pages of the Gospel, *many women, of different ages and conditions,* pass before our eyes. We meet women with illnesses or physical sufferings, such as the one who had "a spirit of infirmity for eighteen years; she was bent over and could not fully straighten herself" (Lk 13:11); or Simon's mother-in-law, who "lay sick with a fever" (Mk 1:30); or the woman "who had a flow of blood" (cf. Mk 5:25–34), who could not touch anyone because it was believed that her touch would make a person "impure." Each of them was healed, and the last-mentioned — the one with a flow of blood, who touched Jesus' garment "in the crowd" (Mk 5:27) — was praised by him for her great faith: "Your faith has made you well" (Mk 5:34). Then there is *the daughter of Jairus,* whom Jesus brings back to life, saying to her tenderly: "Little girl, I say to you, arise" (Mk 5:41). There also is *the widow of Nain,* whose only son Jesus brings back to life, accompanying his action by an expression of

affectionate mercy: "He had compassion on her and said to her, 'Do not weep!'" (Lk 7:13).... There is the *Canaanite woman,* whom Christ extols for her faith, her humility and for that greatness of spirit of which only a mother's heart is capable. "O woman, great is your faith! Be it done for you as you desire" (Mt 15:28). The Canaanite woman was asking for the healing of her daughter....

[And] there is the Samaritan woman, to whom Jesus himself says: "For you have had five husbands, and he whom you now have is not your husband." And she, realizing that he knows the secrets of her life, recognizes him as the Messiah and runs to tell her neighbors. The conversation leading up to this realization is one of the most beautiful in the Gospel (cf. Jn 4:7–27).[321]

Moreover, "the women [were] first at the tomb. They [were] the first to find it empty."[322] To be sure, the women were the only ones who did not lose faith in him.

"Motherhood–Virginity"

Chapter VI discusses the two aspects of a woman's vocation, motherhood and virginity, which brings us back to the Blessed Mother. In Mary, "these *two dimensions of the female vocation* were united in such an exceptional manner, in such a way that one did not exclude the other but wonderfully complemented it."[323]

In fact, the woman plays a special part in the "mutual gift of the [husband and wife] in marriage."[324] Her gift of interior readiness implies a special openness to a new human being, "and this is precisely the woman's 'part.'"[325] The experience of motherhood helps the woman develop her predisposition of paying attention to the other, making a sincere gift of herself.

Man always remains "outside" the process of pregnancy and

birth, and so in many ways he has to learn his own "fatherhood" from the mother. Thus while parenthood is a common responsibility, the "mother's contribution is decisive in laying the foundation for a new human personality."[326]

Motherhood in Mary takes on an even deeper meaning, in that through her motherhood "God begins a New Covenant with humanity."[327] Her motherhood embraces every other mother because "each and every time that *motherhood* is repeated in human history, it is always *related to the Covenant* which God established with the human race through the motherhood of the Mother of God."[328] As John Paul said beautifully, "The history of every human being passes through the threshold of a woman's motherhood."[329]

Just as physical motherhood is a link with the Blessed Mother, so is virginity and celibacy for the sake of the Kingdom. Mary, in whom motherhood was a total gift from God, is the prototype of the new creation because she is a sign of eschatological hope. In other words, Mary is the "beginning and the prototype of a new expectation on the part of all."[330] Through her, "the Gospel puts forward the ideal of the consecration of the person, that is, the person's exclusive dedication to God by virtue of the evangelical counsels: in particular, chastity, poverty, and obedience."[331]

Finally, there is spiritual motherhood, the special place where motherhood and virginity converge. Spiritual motherhood can take on many different forms, in that it manifests itself as concern for various kinds of people, especially the needy. The ways that spiritual motherhood makes itself felt are profoundly personal.

"The Church — The Bride of Christ"

The meditation essentially ends with Chapter VII, "The Church — The Bride of Christ." This section opens with the illustration Saint Paul used in his Letter to the Ephesians comparing the relationship of Christ with the Church to one of husband and wife:

Husbands, love your wives, as Christ loved the

Church and gave himself up for her, that he might sanctify her, having cleansed her by the washing of water with the word, that he might present the Church to himself in splendor, without spot or wrinkle or any such thing, that she might be holy and without blemish. Even so husbands should love their wives as their own bodies. He who loves his wife loves himself. For no man ever hates his own flesh, but nourishes and cherishes it, as Christ does the Church, because we are members of his body. "For this reason, a man shall leave his father and mother and be joined to his wife, and the two shall become one flesh." This is a great mystery, and I mean in reference to Christ and the Church. (5:25–32)

This was nothing new, as the prophets of the Old Testament had used the image of spousal love as a symbol of the Lord's love for his people. Yet in this passage we also find what John Paul called a "Gospel innovation." For it is in the context of Christ's love for his Church, his Bride, that Saint Paul taught that wives must be subject to their husbands and that husbands must love their wives. There is no contradiction here, because the counsel to "be subject" was to be understood and carried out in a new way: as mutual subjection out of love for Christ.[332]

The chapter ends by addressing the question of why the ministerial priesthood is for men only. With the same freedom in which Christ upheld the dignity of women, he also called only men to be his apostles. Christ is the Bridegroom, and the Bridegroom is masculine. There is no ambiguity therefore that the priest acting *in persona Christi* should also be a man. The Church as Bride is also called to give herself totally to Christ. And so, from the times of the early Church, women worked side by side with men through their own charisms and varied service.[333]

It is clear that the Catholic Church, as expressed in these beautiful words of Pope John Paul II, values the heart, mind, and soul of a woman. An appropriate response to anyone who complains that the teachings of the Church denigrate women is, "With all due respect, you are sadly mistaken."

Chapter Six Reflection Questions

Why is it important for us to understand "the reasons for and the consequences of the Creator's decision that the human being should always and only exist as a woman or a man"[334]? What evidence is there that this is an area of confusion today?

Consider the different ways in which secular feminism has negatively impacted our culture. What are the key differences between secular feminism and the "new feminism" proposed by Pope Saint John Paul II? How might living out this new feminism help restore our culture?

What is the role of the laity in the Church and in the world? How do you live this out?

What does it mean to be made in the image and likeness of God? What happens when people do not understand this?

Think of examples that demonstrate how the original sin of Adam and Eve affected men and women differently.

How is it that you find yourself by giving yourself away? Have you found this to be true in your own life?

CHAPTER SEVEN

Love Makes the World Go Round

Pope Benedict XVI, *Deus Caritas Est*

WHAT IS LOVE?

February 11, 2013, was a day of surprises. Pope Benedict XVI announced that he would resign from office, completely shocking the world, particularly the seventy some cardinals who had joined him that morning. They were meeting for an announcement of new canonizations, but the pope had more on his mind than naming new saints. In fact, the meeting had ended, and all who were gathered were getting ready to leave when Benedict asked them to take their seats. Then, he began reading in Latin from a prepared text:

> Dear Brothers,
> I have convoked you to this Consistory, not only for the three canonizations, but also to communicate to you a decision of great importance for the life of the Church. After having repeatedly examined my conscience before God, I have come to the certainty that

my strengths, due to an advanced age, are no longer suited to an adequate exercise of the Petrine ministry. I am well aware that this ministry, due to its essential spiritual nature, must be carried out not only with words and deeds, but no less with prayer and suffering. However, in today's world, subject to so many rapid changes and shaken by questions of deep relevance for the life of faith, in order to govern the barque of Saint Peter and proclaim the Gospel, both strength of mind and body are necessary, strength which in the last few months, has deteriorated in me to the extent that I have had to recognize my incapacity to adequately fulfill the ministry entrusted to me. For this reason, and well aware of the seriousness of this act, with full freedom I declare that I renounce the ministry of Bishop of Rome, Successor of Saint Peter, entrusted to me by the Cardinals on 19 April 2005, in such a way, that as from 28 February 2013, at 20:00 hours, the See of Rome, the See of Saint Peter, will be vacant and a Conclave to elect the new Supreme Pontiff will have to be convoked by those whose competence it is.

Dear Brothers, I thank you most sincerely for all the love and work with which you have supported me in my ministry and I ask pardon for all my defects. And now, let us entrust the Holy Church to the care of Our Supreme Pastor, Our Lord Jesus Christ, and implore his holy Mother Mary, so that she may assist the Cardinal Fathers with her maternal solicitude, in electing a new Supreme Pontiff. With regard to myself, I wish to also devotedly serve the Holy Church of God in the future through a life dedicated to prayer.

From the Vatican, 10 February 2013
BENEDICTUS PP XVI[335]

Cardinal Francis Arinze was in the audience that day, and he shared his reaction to this historic announcement in an interview several days later. In it, he reminds us of one of life's most important lessons: Christ is the only constant in this life:

> It was like thunder; the announcement came without advance warning.... When he had read a few sentences, I began to suspect where he was going....
>
> I said to myself, the Pope is teaching us all something very important by this act. One of the titles of the Pope is "Servant of the servants of God." We come and go. Any of us can go, only Christ does not go. Without Christ, the Church loses its foundation, its direction, its harmony. Popes come and go, bishops come and go, and so do politicians.[336]

Pope Benedict came and went, but not without leaving behind a long and lasting legacy. Over his eight-year pontificate, he produced three encyclicals, completed his trilogy on Jesus of Nazareth, and wrote thousands of addresses, papal documents, as well as hallmark homilies, which were known to "cool the mind and warm the heart."[337] The consummate teacher, one might argue that everything regarding his papacy was about teaching, including his actions, right up to his shocking resignation.

In the truest sense of the word, Pope Benedict XVI was (and still is) a son of the Church. Joseph Aloisius Ratzinger was born on Holy Saturday, April 16, 1927, in a small Upper Bavarian town, Marktl am Inn, nestled in the foothills of the Alps. He grew up in a devout Catholic family, embedded in the culture of Bavarian Catholicism. He liked to say, "In my vocation, I belong to the world, but my heart beats Bavarian."[338]

Joseph and his older brother, Georg, were both ordained to the priesthood on June 29, 1951, on a magnificent summer day that he would always remember as "the high point of my life."[339]

Two years later, Father Joseph Ratzinger received a doctorate in theology, and from there he proceeded to teach at several German universities.

He was still young, only thirty-five, when, in 1962, he became an adviser to one of Europe's most influential bishops, Cardinal Joseph Frings of Cologne, Germany, at the Second Vatican Council. Already considered one of the world's leading theologians, Ratzinger emerged as the most articulate voice of the authentic teaching of the council.[340] While he was a powerful presence to his fellow theologians, he also became a presence for the whole Church, speaking plain sense at a time when nonsense abounded.

Just seven years later, in 1969, in the midst of the turbulent years that followed the council, Professor Joseph Ratzinger gave a radio talk with the provocative title, "What Will the Future Church Look Like?" While he is no soothsayer, the story has been repeated many times, as the gist of it continues to unfold:

> From the crisis of today a new Church of tomorrow will emerge — a Church that has lost much. She will become small and will have to start afresh more or less from the beginning. She will no longer be able to inhabit many of the edifices she built in prosperity. As the number of her adherents diminishes, so she will lose many of her social privileges.
>
> In contrast to an earlier age, she will be seen much more as a voluntary society, entered only be free decision.... But in all [this] ... the Church will find her essence afresh and with full conviction in that which was always at her center: faith in the triune God, in Jesus Christ, the son of God made man, in the presence of the Spirit until the end of the world.[341]

While Ratzinger loved being a university professor, he gave it up when Pope Paul VI appointed him archbishop of Munich, West Germany, in May 1977. Less than a month later, Paul VI elevated Archbishop Ratzinger to the College of Cardinals.

Over the years, particularly during his pontificate, Pope Benedict reminded the world that God, in the person of Jesus Christ, is an ever-present reality. He preached that rejection of God could only lead to catastrophe. Benedict was critical of modern-day secularism, and he protested against being trapped in a world where there is no such thing as truth, where everything is allowed, and nothing has any meaning.

In 1981, Pope John Paul II tapped him to serve as the prefect of the Congregation for the Doctrine of the Faith (CDF), the Vatican office responsible for promoting and upholding Catholic doctrine. (Beginning in 2001, the CDF has also had jurisdiction over clergy sex abuse cases.) This post earned him the names "God's Rottweiler" and "the Panzer Cardinal," a nod to both his German heritage and the caricature of him as an arch-conservative. Despite this it was clear that he had a brilliant and open mind that surpassed these crude labels. In an age of unbalanced thinking, his thought stood out for its harmony and integrity. As prefect, he became one of Pope John Paul's closest collaborators. This allowed him to become a major figure on the Vatican stage for a quarter of a century.

In addition to countless other duties, he supervised the writing of many official documents on issues of the day, ranging from bioethics and homosexuality to liberation theology and the obligations of Catholic politicians and citizens. He denounced Marxism and its utopian vision for social change. Similarly, he rejected the views of some theologians who sought to undermine the Faith by placing it on the same level as other religions.[342]

As the years passed and he began to age, there were rumors that Cardinal Ratzinger was going to retire. He admitted that he had wanted to retire in 1991, 1996, and 2001, so that he could write books and return to his studies. Yet seeing the example of Pope John Paul II, who was still giving his entire self to his God and his Church, Ratzinger determined that retiring was something he could not do. He must continue.

Everything changed for Joseph Ratzinger on April 2, 2005, with the death of Pope John Paul II. Six days later, as dean of the College of Cardinals, Cardinal Ratzinger was the main celebrant of the funeral for the beloved pontiff, a funeral that was transformed into one on the most stunning events in human history. It was appropriately tagged "the human event of a generation."[343] More than two billion people participated, either in person or by watching it on television, to say goodbye to this giant of a man.

Ratzinger's powerful homily received a spontaneous and prolonged standing ovation. He "had moved them deeply, and not by theatrics but by a solid catechesis, winsome and challenging at the same time."[344] For anyone who had eyes to see, the cardinal's future was about to change. The idea of a Ratzinger papacy was becoming a real possibility. He celebrated his seventy-eighth birthday on April 16, admitting to a few of his friends that he was becoming "somewhat nervous" that the guillotine might fall upon him. If that happened, he would be the oldest cardinal to become pope since 1730.[345]

Two days later, on April 18, 2005, he opened the conclave with another powerful homily, speaking about the trivialization of evil and the different ideological currents running through the Church, including Marxism, liberalism, individualism, and mysticism. He spoke of a relativism that permitted one to be "tossed here and there," carried about by every wind of doctrine. Finally, he spoke about an adult faith deeply rooted in friendship with Christ.[346]

This was not a campaign speech. Joseph Ratzinger never desired to become pope. He "had often described himself as 'the man of the second row,' a supporter rather than a leader."[347] Others thought differently, however, and he was elected pope on the fourth ballot in one of the shortest conclaves in history. He had no choice other than to accept. When asked what name he would take, he chose Benedict. He would be Pope Benedict XVI.

Several years later, in 2010, he told his biographer, Peter See-wald: "I had been so sure that this office was not my calling, but that God would now grant me some peace and quiet after strenuous years. But then I could only say, explain to myself: God's will is apparently otherwise and something new and completely different is beginning for me. He will be with me."[348]

Indeed, God *was* with him, from the first day of his pontificate until the last. How else to explain the beauty of the written word found in his encyclicals, especially *Deus Caritas Est* ("God is Love")? Written just over eight months after his election, this letter was "Pope Benedict's attempt to introduce, or in some cases reintroduce, the world to 'the God with a human face,' which is the face of crucified love."[349]

When asked why he chose love as the theme of his first encyclical, Pope Benedict replied:

> Today the word "love" is so tarnished, so spoiled and so abused, that one is almost afraid to pronounce it with one's lips. And yet it is a primordial word, expression of the primordial reality; we cannot simply abandon it, we must take it up again, purify it, and give back to it its original splendor so that it might illuminate our life and lead it on the right path. This awareness led me to choose love as the theme of my first encyclical.
>
> [The encyclical seeks to] underline the centrality of faith in God, in that God who has assumed a human face and a human heart. Faith is not a theory that one can take up or lay aside. It is something very concrete: It is the criterion that decides our lifestyle. In an age in which hostility and greed have become superpowers, an age in which we witness the abuse of religion to the point of culminating in

hatred, neutral rationality on its own is unable to protect us. We are in need of the living God who has loved us unto death.[350]

Obviously, this message is not new. But in a world beset by violence, threats of intimidation, and exploitation of the weak and vulnerable, this encyclical is truly good news.

DEUS CARITAS EST

Signed on Christmas Day 2005, Pope Benedict's first encyclical set the tone for his pontificate. Recognizing the greatest evils our culture faces, particularly when it comes to sex and human dignity, Pope Benedict XVI wanted to begin his papacy by clarifying this most important of all words, "love."

This encyclical letter is divided into two main sections. Part I, "The Unity of Love in Creation and in Salvation History," focuses on philosophical ideas about the nature of love, examining the nature of God's love for us, and the intrinsic link between Divine and human love. Part II, "The Practice of Love by the Church as a 'Community of Love,'" looks at "love in action," highlighting charity as a responsibility of the Church, the interrelationship between justice and love, and the distinguishing characteristics of the charitable actions of the Church.

"The Unity of Love in Creation and in Salvation History"

The encyclical opens with a passage from the First Letter of John: "God is love, and he who abides in love abides in God, and God abides in him" (1 Jn 4:16). These opening words express the core of the Christian faith, and they tell us everything we need to know about God, for everything that God is and everything that he does is love. This is so comforting, particularly "in a world in which God's Name is sometimes linked with revenge or even with hatred and violence. The Christian message of God-Love is very timely."[351]

Today, "love" has become one of the most frequently used and misused words, attached to a number of quite different meanings.[352] The problem is one of language, and it lies in the fact that there is only one word ("love") that encompasses many types of love:

> God's love for us is fundamental for our lives, and it raises important questions about who God is and who we are. In considering this, we immediately find ourselves hampered by a problem of language....
>
> Let us first of all bring to mind the vast semantic range of the word "love": we speak of love of country, love of one's profession, love between friends, love of work, love between parents and children, love between family members, love of neighbor and love of God. Amid this multiplicity of meanings, however, one in particular stands out: love between man and woman, where body and soul are inseparably joined and human beings glimpse an apparently irresistible promise of happiness. This would seem to be the very epitome of love; all other kinds of love immediately seem to fade in comparison. So we need to ask: are all these forms of love basically one, so that love, in its many and varied manifestations, is ultimately a single reality, or are we merely using the same word to designate totally different realities?[353]

In order to address this issue of language, Pope Benedict XVI, ever the professor, looked back to the ancient Greek philosophers, who played a pivotal role in the development of our understanding of the nature of love. There are three basic kinds of love in the Christian tradition: friendship love, known by its Greek name, *philia*; the human passion of love, known by its Greek name, *eros*; and Divine love, charity (from the Latin *caritas*), also known by its Greek name, *agape*.

Friendship love, *philia*, is the outgrowth of our natural human desire for communion. As we mature, it inspires us gradually to widen our circle of love to include extended family members and friends. It is a virtuous love, characterized by steadfast loyalty, deep affection, and mutual trust.

What is often referred to today as romantic love was called *eros* by the ancient Greeks. It is the highly charged, passionate, sensual love, often seen in young lovers. It is "that love between man and woman which is neither planned nor willed, but somehow imposes itself upon human beings."[354] If we are not careful to govern our desires, *eros* can be destructive; at the very least, it does not last. In fact, *eros* often has a negative connotation, but, as this letter demonstrates, *eros* can be purified of its negative meaning when it is integrated with the highest form of love, charity, in the life of Jesus Christ.

The type of love which is mentioned most frequently in the New Testament is *agape*. This type of love goes beyond the limits of *philia* and *eros*. Its character clearly points "to something new and distinct about the Christian understanding of love."[355] *Agape* is the embodiment of love; it is a self-sacrificing love, the archetype against which all other love is measured.

Agape is what we have come to understand as the essence of divine love, or charity. This is the type of love that Jesus referred to in the Gospel of John: "A new commandment I give to you, that you love one another; even as I have loved you, that you also love one another. By this all men will know that you are my disciples, if you have love for one another" (Jn 13:34–35).

Over the course of history, there have been critics who have condemned the Christian understanding of love as prudish, naive, and unrealistic. For them, Christian morality is repressive, nothing more than a set of rules and regulations that would prevent people from indulging in the pleasures of life. Friedrich Nietzsche, a nineteenth-century German philosopher, was one such critic. Nietzsche opposed Christianity and disparaged past philosophers for their blind acceptance of Christian morality, suggesting that it was repressive and responsible for taking the fun out of human sexuality.

So, *Deus Caritas Est* tackles the question, "Did Christianity really destroy *eros*?"[356] To find the answer, we can simply take a closer look at the pre-Christian world, which, in fact, does not support Nietzsche's point of view. The concept of "sacred" prostitution and the divinization of *eros* as practiced in Greek culture did not result in an experience of supreme happiness. Rather, it was a perversion of religion, a means to exploit and debase the prostitutes who served in the temple.[357] In fact, when *eros* gives in to the temptation to reduce a person to a mere object of sensual need or desire, when it uses the person in a utilitarian way for the selfish satisfaction of personal pleasure, it loses its dignity and its grandeur. "An intoxicated and undisciplined *eros* … is not an ascent in 'ecstasy' towards the Divine, but a fall, a degradation of man."[358]

Eros, which is implanted in human nature by God himself, needs discipline, purification, and growth in maturity if it is not to lose its original dignity or degenerate into pure "sex," thus causing one or both partners to become a commodity. In other words, when *eros* is ruled by the conscious decisions of our human intellect and will, we are capable of rising above ourselves and our sinful inclinations. When we work to discipline and purify *eros*, it can provide the image and foretaste of the Divine, "that beatitude for which our whole being yearns."[359]

Eros is a love that encompasses our entire being, body and soul,[360] because our bodies and souls are not separate entities. "Though made of body and soul, man is one."[361] It is not possible for us to isolate our physical actions from our inner selves. In fact, what we do "to" and "with" our bodies, we necessarily also do to and with our souls. For this reason, *eros* and *agape* need to be connected to each other. Even if *eros* is at first only a desire, in drawing near to the other person it becomes less and less concerned with itself and increasingly seeks the happiness of the other. It is then that the element of *agape* enters into this love.

It is only when both dimensions — body and soul — are united that man attains his full stature:[362]

> Nowadays Christianity of the past is often criticized as having been opposed to the body; and it is quite true that tendencies of this sort have always existed. Yet the contemporary way of exalting the body is deceptive. *Eros*, reduced to pure "sex," has become a commodity, a mere "thing" to be bought and sold, or rather, man himself becomes a commodity. This is hardly man's great "yes" to the body. On the contrary, he now considers his body and his sexuality as the purely material part of himself, to be used and exploited at will. Nor does he see it as an arena for the exercise of his freedom, but as a mere object that he attempts, as he pleases, to make both enjoyable and harmless. Here we are actually dealing with a debasement of the human body: no longer is it integrated into our overall existential freedom; no longer is it a vital expression of our whole being, but it is more or less relegated to the purely biological sphere.[363]

In essence, only when our body and soul are united can love become the stage where we are able to exercise our freedom.[364] This unity frees us from our passions, frees us to love, to make a gift of our self to the one whom we love, and to avoid sin.

It is tempting to simplify our understanding of *eros* and *agape* too much, seeing *agape* as noble and elevated, while *eros* is looked at with suspicion and possibly even rejected as unworthy. The problem with this way of thinking is that it completely detaches the essence of Christianity from the reality of our human relationships.

While *agape* and *eros* are distinct, they can never be completely separated. "'Love' is a single reality, but with different dimensions; at different times, one or other dimension may emerge more clearly."[365] Thus the fulfillment of both *eros* and *agape* is brought about "the more the two, in their different aspects, find a proper unity in the one reality of love."[366]

Because of our natural tendency toward sin, we are always in danger of confusing the pleasure of infatuation with authentic love. If pleasure becomes the goal of our relationship instead of the means through which our love has the opportunity to mature and deepen into an authentic reflection of Divine love, "*eros* is impoverished and even loses its own nature."[367] Then, instead of finding happiness, we feel empty and used. People are not objects to be used by others as the means to an end. In God's plan of love, "the value of the person is always greater than the value of pleasure."[368]

This is why, "from the standpoint of creation, *eros* directs man towards marriage, to a bond which is unique and definitive; thus, and only thus, does it fulfill its deepest purpose."[369] It is in marriage that *eros* finds its truest fulfillment and meaning. Here in the sacrament of love, human passion is elevated and ennobled, going beyond the limitations of mere physical attraction and desire.

It is in Jesus Christ, the incarnate love of God, that *eros* and *agape* come together in the most radical form of love. In dying on the cross, by giving himself in order to raise and save man, Jesus expressed love in its most sublime form. God's great passionate love for us is not just *agape*, it is *eros* in its perfection. God is always searching and longing for us:

It is God himself who goes in search of the "stray

sheep," a suffering and lost humanity. When Jesus speaks in his parables of the shepherd who goes after the lost sheep, of the woman who looks for the lost coin, of the father who goes to meet and embrace his prodigal son, these are no mere words: they constitute an explanation of his very being and activity. His death on the Cross is the culmination of that turning of God against himself in which he gives himself in order to raise man up and save him. *This is love in its most radical form.*[370]

Moreover, "he guaranteed an enduring presence of this oblative act through the institution of the Eucharist, in which he gives himself under the species of bread and wine as a new manna that unites us with him."[371] Here, we are all united with him, and at the same time, we are united with all the others to whom he gives himself. We all become "one body" in Christ.

Thanks to this encounter with the *agape* of God, love of neighbor and love of God are truly united, and the commandment to "love one another; even as I have loved you" (Jn 13:34) is no longer solely a precept. Indeed, "love can be 'commanded' because it has first been given."[372] In other words, "since [God] 'loved us first,' love can also blossom as a response within us."[373] "His friend is my friend."[374] Thus, by its very nature, love must be shared with others, as "love grows through love."[375] And, only by "seeing with the eyes of Christ, can [we] give to others much more than their outward necessities; [we] can give them the look of love which they crave."[376]

"The Practice of Love by the Church as a 'Community of Love'"

Part II of *Deus Caritas Est* looks to the community of believers, the Church. Not only do the members of the Church have a responsibility to and for others, they also have a responsibility for the entire Church, which must reflect the love of God in its charitable activity:

> The entire activity of the Church is an expression of a love that seeks the integral good of man: it seeks his evangelization through Word and Sacrament, an undertaking that is often heroic in the way it is acted out in history; and it seeks to promote man in the various arenas of life and human activity. Love is therefore the service that the Church carries out in order to attend constantly to man's sufferings and his needs, including material needs. And this is the aspect, this *service of charity*, on which I want to focus in the second part of the Encyclical.[377]

In addition to proclaiming the Word of God and celebrating the sacraments, *agape* love is part of the very fabric of the Church. For the Church, "charity is not a kind of welfare activity which could equally well be left to others, but it is part of her nature, an indispensable expression of her very being. The Church is God's family in the world. [And], in this family, no one ought to go without the necessities of life."[378]

Sadly, not everyone agrees with this assessment. Since the time of the Industrial Revolution in the nineteenth century, many have raised a fundamental objection regarding the Church's charitable activity: they claim that this type of charity is opposed to justice, and that it is only a means of maintaining the status quo.

The thinking here is that the Church's individual works of charity do not address the root problems of poverty and oppression. Instead, they foster unjust systems by making them appear tolerable, which then slows down the potential evolution of a better world. Mother Teresa was frequently criticized for this. She took care of the dying, rather than trying to fix the reason behind their death.

This was the mindset of Karl Marx. He fostered atheism, revolution, and class warfare as a way to solve the injustices that he observed in the factories during the Industrial Revolution. Yet the truth is, the just ordering of society and of the state is a core duty of the state and therefore cannot be an immediate responsibility of the Church:

> Love — *caritas* — will always prove necessary, even in the most just society. There is no ordering of the State so just that it can eliminate the need for a service of love. Whoever wants to eliminate love is preparing to eliminate man as such. There will always be suffering which cries out for consolation and help. There will always be loneliness. There will always be situations of material need where help in the form of concrete love of neighbor is indispensable. The State, which would provide everything, absorbing everything into itself, would ultimately become a mere bureaucracy incapable of guaranteeing the very thing which the suffering person — every person — needs: namely, loving personal concern.[379]

The pope continues: "In all humility we will do what we can, and in all humility we will entrust the rest to the Lord. It is God who governs the world, not we. We offer him our service only to the extent that we can, and for as long as he grants us the strength."[380]

Pope Benedict brings the beautiful reflection to a close by encouraging us to always let love be our light: "Love is the light — and in the end, the only light — that can always illuminate a world grown dim and give us the courage needed to keep living and working. Love is possible, and we are able to practice it because we are created in the image of God. To experience love and in this way [is] to cause the light of God to enter into the world."[381]

Chapter Seven Reflection Questions

If you could think of one thing that would heal our culture, what would it be? If it were up to you, where would you begin?

Consider then-Cardinal Ratzinger's ideas about the future of the Church. How is this playing out in our world today?

Why is the message of God's love so powerful and why are so many people today afraid of it?

In the normal course of human relationships, we are first attracted to others by certain qualities or characteristics that we perceive in them, regardless of whether our perceptions are grounded in reality. With this in mind, does *eros* always have to precede *agape*? Can we love someone we are not attracted to?

Consider why the Church's charitable activities are not opposed to justice and think of some examples that prove this.

How can government "womb-to-tomb" social services, medical care, and pension systems stifle the human and Christian instinct to reach out in solidarity to the suffering "other"?

CHAPTER EIGHT

A Tale of Two Synods

Francis, *Amoris Laetitia*

A NEW KIND OF POPE

From the moment Pope Francis (Jorge Mario Bergoglio) stepped onto the loggia on March 13, 2013, looking like the proverbial deer caught in the headlights, it was clear that he was different. Instead of smilingly jubilantly with arms extended, as did the three previous pontiffs, the new pope initially gave the world a faint smile and a timid wave. It was this first impression that prompted a popular Catholic blogger to predict that one day he might be invoked as "Pope Francis, future patron saint of the socially awkward."[382]

That first impression quickly dissipated, however, as the world came to see that this is a man comfortable in his own skin. A native of Argentina, Jorge Bergoglio wears old black shoes, rides the bus, and pays his own hotel tab. The newly elected pope would also choose to reside in Suite 201 of the *Domus Sanctae Marthae*, simple living quarters for visiting clergy to the Vatican, foregoing the tradition of living in the papal apartments.

Pope Francis kisses babies, shakes hands, and on the day of his inaugural Mass he spontaneously left the popemobile to embrace and bless a severely disabled man. He is always approaching people and hugging them, engaging in conversation, sharing funny anecdotes. As the founder of a religious community in northern Italy observed, Francis is "the pope becomes man."[383]

From the beginning of his pontificate, Francis has made it clear that he wants a Church "that is not just top-down, but also horizontal."[384] He explained his thinking in the 2013 apostolic exhortation *Evangelii Gaudium* ("The Joy of the Gospel"):

> Nor do I believe that the papal magisterium should be expected to offer a definitive or complete word on every question which affects the Church and the world. It is not advisable for the Pope to take the place of local Bishops in the discernment of every issue which arises in their territory. In this sense, I am conscious of the need to promote a sound "decentralization."[385]

Within a month Francis created a council of eight cardinals (referred to as the C8) from across the world to advise him in the governance of the universal Church and to plan the reform of the Roman Curia, a project that Pope Francis was (and still is) eager to implement. With their help, Francis immediately began overhauling the "centralist, monarchic model of the Vatican."[386] What the pope wants is "a collegial movement in the Church, where all the issues can be brought up, and afterwards, he can make a decision."[387]

To implement this idea, Pope Francis developed a plan. In October 2013, he announced that the 2015 ordinary Synod of Bishops,[388] which was already scheduled to discuss "The Pastoral Challenges of the Family in the Context of Evangelization," would be preceded by an extraordinary synod[389] in October 2014. The plan was to have this extraordinary synod decide the discussion points for the 2015 synod. Additionally, in between the two synods, the faithful would be given the opportunity to offer their views on various issues based on their lived experience and prayerful reflection.

Pope Francis' plan was set in motion. In October 2013, an extensive questionnaire was sent to national bishops' conferences across the world, with instructions to ask ordinary Catholics what they thought of the Church's teaching on the family. The questionnaire, which some bishops' conferences put online for Catholics to answer directly, did not shy away from controversial issues such as premarital sex, contraception, divorce, remarriage, same-sex relationships, in vitro fertilization, and adoption by gay couples.

Asking lay people to participate in the questionnaire was revolutionary.[390] In his book, *Pope Francis: The Struggle for the Soul of Catholicism*, British author Paul Vallely explains what happened next:

> As the months passed, the results of the questionnaire began to leak to the media, despite requests from the Curia that they should be passed on to Rome without being published. Bishops in some countries had refused to issue the survey to their flock; in Italy, for example, they had done almost nothing to engage ordinary Catholics with the questions. But it gradually became clear that in many of the 114 countries that had replied — from Germany and Ireland to the Philippines and Japan — a tectonic gap had opened between official teaching and what Catholics in the pew believe and do. The Canadian bishops respected the Vatican request not to publish the details but announced that their survey had found "a huge gap" between theory and practice.[391]

Upon reviewing the survey results, Pope Francis made it clear that he wanted the lived experience of lay Catholics to be the starting point of the extraordinary synod. Their views were to be the basis for the *instrumentum laboris*, the working document on which the approaching synod would be based.

Francis was not finished. In February 2014, he invited German Cardinal Walter Kasper to speak to a group of cardinals who were gathered to discuss the two forthcoming synods on the family. Kasper is a well-known proponent of changing the Church's teaching regarding access to Communion for the divorced and civilly remarried.

The cardinal's talk was extremely controversial. An impassioned discussion followed, "with heavyweight conservatives lining up against the German advocate for reform."[392] Francis rejoiced in the exchange: "'The cardinals knew that they could say what they wanted, and they presented different points of view, which are always enriching. Open and fraternal dialogue fosters the growth of theological and pastoral thought,' he said, 'I am not afraid of this; on the contrary, I seek it.'"[393]

Anyone who followed the 2014 synod knows that it was indeed extraordinary. Author Mary Jo Anderson described it in an article entitled, "What I Saw at the Synod and What It Means for 2015":

> This Extraordinary Synod had controversy — and some intrigue — aired in both the Catholic and the secular press. You know the issues that remain after this preliminary Synod include these tender questions: How shall the Church speak with pastoral care to the divorced and civilly remarried? What hope should we offer to those with homosexual inclinations?
>
> Already some insist that the Synod was hijacked and will forever be known as the Synod for the Divorced and the Gay. Others believe they witnessed

the Holy Spirit throw a coup into confusion; wherein the proponents of "opening" to the divorced and remarried and gay unions were knocked on their heels by Synod fathers who refused to submit to their machinations.[394]

Similarly, George Weigel shared his thoughts about the 2015 ordinary synod in an article called "What Really Happened at Synod 2015":

> Real issues were debated, with real consequences at stake. Some of this was visible atop the froth of the mainstream media and blogosphere commentary. How would the Catholic Church settle the argument, launched by Cardinal Walter Kasper in February 2014, about its long-standing and doctrinally informed discipline of not admitting the divorced and civilly remarried to Holy Communion?...
> [How did] that bear on the relationship between mercy and truth, between pastoral accompaniment and pastoral challenge, between one's condition of life and one's ability to receive the grace of the sacraments?
>
> The fact that, for the first time in two thousand years, the Catholic Church is "catholic" (universal, global) in an existential sense put other important questions in play. How should the experience of the young churches of Africa, where the idea of marriage and family is received as a liberating force, be weighed against the experience of dying churches in which divorce is as widespread as Sunday Mass attendance is not, churches whose leaders claimed before the synod that Catholicism's teaching on divorce drives people away from God?[395]

From all of this flows Pope Francis' post-synodal apostolic exhortation, *Amoris Laetitia* ("The Joy of Love"). According to theologian Dr. Timothy O'Malley of Notre Dame, "it is this remarkable theological and social vision of the sacrament of marriage that may come to be Pope Francis' great contribution to the Church."[396]

To be sure, Pope Francis' exhortation on love and marriage is markedly different than the encyclical Pope Leo XIII wrote on basically the same topic nearly 140 years earlier. As we saw earlier in this book, when God allowed Pope Leo to look into the future, it shook him to the core. He immediately invoked the intercession of Saint Michael the Archangel to watch over the Church and the people of God.

Pope Francis is living Pope Leo's vision. Consequently, while Church teachings have remained the same, Francis needs to make them accessible to the people of today, to the very same people who rejected Pope Paul's *Humanae Vitae* and who are now living in the messy world that he predicted. Pope Francis longs for the souls that have been lost along the way, and he is eager and willing to open every door doctrinally possible to bring them back into the arms of Our Lady, who will forever be the mother of the Church.

AMORIS LAETITIA

To understand Pope Francis, we first have to understand one of his favorite phrases: "Time is greater than space." To date, this curious expression is found in all of his teaching documents, including *Amoris Laetitia*. More than just an unusual choice of words, it is a fundamental principle of his. It is also key to understanding his reason for writing this "Synod-summarizing"[397] exhortation.

This is how the pope explains what he means by "time is greater than space":

This principle enables us to work slowly but surely,

without being obsessed with immediate results. It helps us patiently to endure difficult and adverse situations, or inevitable changes in our plans. It invites us to accept the tension between fullness and limitation, and to give a priority to time. One of the faults which we occasionally observe in sociopolitical activity is that spaces and power are preferred to time and processes. Giving priority to space means madly attempting to keep everything together in the present, trying to possess all the spaces of power and of self-assertion; it is to crystallize processes and presume to hold them back. Giving priority to time means being concerned about initiating processes rather than possessing spaces.[398]

In other words, according to Deacon Jim Russell of the Archdiocese of St. Louis:

Our Holy Father is a process-starter and *not* a space-dominator. And all the hand-wringing in the world is not going to budge him an inch closer to dominating "spaces" by simply — and statically — issuing additional "space-filling" decrees or re-statements of existing teaching or practice (such as, for example, the non-reception of Holy Communion by the divorced-remarried-not-annulled). That's just not what he does or even *tries* to do. Clearly, *Amoris Laetitia* is a "process-building" document — it's a summary of the two-year-long Synodal *process*. It's not an attempt to fill spaces.[399]

According to Pope Francis himself, the purpose of *Amoris Laetitia* is to present "the full ideal of marriage, God's plan in all its grandeur."[400] It "is a serene, peaceful reflection on the beauty of love, how to educate the children, to prepare for marriage.... It emphasizes responsibilities that could be developed by the Pontifical Council for the Laity in the form of guidelines."[401]

A striking feature of *Amoris Laetitia* is its length. "It is some three times longer than Saint John Paul II's 1981 apostolic exhortation *Familiaris Consortio* that similarly resulted from a synod on marriage and family."[402] One reason for the size of the document is that it is the fruit of, essentially, a two-year synod. There is much to process, therefore Francis took his time, just as any father would for the good of his children:

> In this document, we hear clearly Pope Francis' voice as a pastor — a voice that is different from his two more scholarly predecessors. As a pastor, he gives couples an array of wise practical advice, ranging from communication and conflict resolution, to building and sustaining intimacy, to aging together, to navigating crises or dealing with old wounds.[403]

Francis has insisted he is not changing or modifying the Church's doctrine on marriage. "But he clearly does want to change the tone in which that teaching is heard."[404] This is an idea to which he returns repeatedly in the document:

> "The Church must be particularly concerned to offer understanding, comfort and acceptance, rather than imposing straightaway a set of rules that only lead people to feel judged and abandoned by the very Mother called to show them God's mercy. Rather than offering the healing power of grace and the light of the Gospel message, some would 'indoctrinate' that message, turning it into 'dead stones to be hurled at others.'"[405]

Introduction

First of all, there is good news to share about marriage and family: for all the many signs of crisis in the institution of marriage, "the desire to marry and form a family remains vibrant, especially among young people, and this is an inspiration to the Church."[406] Moreover, "as a response to that desire, 'the Christian proclamation on the family is good news indeed.'"[407]

The synod process provided an opportunity to discuss a wide range of topics regarding the situation of the family in today's world, and "the complexity of the issues that arose revealed the need for continued open discussion on a number of doctrinal, moral, spiritual, and pastoral questions."[408] There are problems aplenty, but not everything can be solved with one broad brush:

> Since "time is greater than space," I would make it clear that not all discussions of doctrinal, moral or pastoral issues need to be settled by interventions of the magisterium. Unity of teaching and practice is certainly necessary in the Church, but this does not preclude various ways of interpreting some aspects of that teaching or drawing certain consequences from it. This will always be the case as the Spirit guides us towards the entire truth (cf. Jn 16:13), until he leads us fully into the mystery of Christ and enables us to see all things as he does. Each country or region, moreover, can seek solutions better suited to its culture and sensitive to its traditions and local needs. For "cultures are in fact quite diverse and every general principle ... needs to be enculturated, if it is to be respected and applied."[409]

In the Light of the Word

Chapter One is inspired by Sacred Scripture, recounting the many different families found in the Old and New Testaments. "The Bible is full of families, births, love stories and family crises. This is true from its very first page, with the appearance of Adam and Eve's family with all its burden of violence but also its enduring strength (cf. Gn 4) to its very last page, where we behold the wedding feast of the Bride and the Lamb (Rv 21:2,9)."[410] We should reflect on the family not as some abstract ideal but as a practical reality. From the beginning of time, the family has been confronted with sin, which turned love into domination. This has since been replayed in every family, in every generation.

The Experiences and Challenges of Families

Chapter Two considers the current situation of families while drawing heavily on the final reports from the two synods. Today's families are facing immense challenges, everything from "migration to the ideological denial of differences between the sexes ('ideology of gender'); from the culture of the provisional to the anti-birth mentality and the impact of biotechnology in the field of procreation; from the lack of housing and work to pornography and abuse of minors; from inattention to persons with disabilities, to lack of respect for the elderly; from the legal dismantling of the family, to violence against women."[411]

In order to appropriately address these issues and others, there have been "countless studies [that] have been made of marriage and the family, their current problems and challenges."[412] This document, however, will focus on "concrete realities":

> The humility of realism helps us to avoid presenting "a far too abstract and almost artificial theological ideal of marriage, far removed from the concrete situations and practical possibilities of real families." Idealism does not allow marriage to be understood for what it is, that is, a "dynamic path to personal development and fulfillment." It is unrealistic to think that families can sustain themselves

"simply by stressing doctrinal, bioethical and moral issues, without encouraging openness to grace."[413]

The root of many of the challenges that families now experience is rampant individualism, so prevalent today:

> "The tensions created by an overly individualistic culture, caught up with possessions and pleasures, leads to intolerance and hostility in families." Here I would also include today's fast pace of life, stress and the organization of society and labor, since all these are cultural factors which militate against permanent decisions....
>
> The ideal of marriage, marked by a commitment to exclusivity and stability, is swept aside whenever it proves inconvenient or tiresome. The fear of loneliness and the desire for stability and fidelity exist side by side with a growing fear of entrapment in a relationship that could hamper the achievement of one's personal goals.[414]

Looking to Jesus: The Vocation of the Family

Chapter Three truly depicts the vocation of the family as depicted in the Gospel and affirmed by the Church over time. Above all, it emphasizes the themes of indissolubility, the sacramental nature of marriage, the transmission of life, and the education of children, liberally quoting Pope Benedict XVI, Pope John Paul II, and Pope Paul VI, thus demonstrating the continuity of the Church's teachings on these particular issues.

Drawing extensively from the Final Report of the 2015 synod, this chapter also touches on "imperfect situations":

> Seeing things with the eyes of Christ inspires the Church's pastoral care for the faithful who are living

together, or are only married civilly, or are divorced
and remarried. Following this divine pedagogy, the
Church turns with love to those who participate in
her life in an imperfect manner: she seeks the grace
of conversion for them; she encourages them to do
good, to take loving care of each other and to serve
the community in which they live and work....
When a couple in an irregular union attains a note-
worthy stability through a public bond — and is
characterized by deep affection, responsibility towards the children and the ability to overcome tri-
als — this can be seen as an opportunity, where
possible, to lead them to celebrate the Sacrament of
Matrimony....

Therefore, while clearly stating the Church's
teaching, pastors are to avoid judgments that do
not take into account the complexity of various situations, and they are to be attentive, by necessity, to
how people experience and endure distress because
of their condition.[415]

Love in Marriage

Chapter Four is stunningly beautiful, celebrating the love between
a husband and a wife. It has been called an "extremely rich and
valuable contribution to Christian married life, unprecedented in
previous papal documents."[416] The chapter begins:

All that has been said so far would be insufficient
to express the Gospel of marriage and the family,
were we not also to speak of love. For we cannot
encourage a path of fidelity and mutual self-giving
without encouraging the growth, strengthening and
deepening of conjugal and family love. Indeed, the
grace of the sacrament of marriage is intended be-

fore all else "to perfect the couple's love."[417]

Next, the document turns to Saint Paul's "Hymn to Charity":[418] "Love is patient and is kind; love is not jealous or boastful; it is not arrogant or rude. Love does not insist on its own way; it is not irritable or resentful; it does not rejoice at wrong, but rejoices in the right. Love bears all things, believes all things, hopes all things, endures all things" (1 Cor 13:4–7). *Amoris Laetitia* unpacks each of these passages, "carefully and tenderly describing human love in absolutely concrete terms."[419]

It is not possible to review each of these passages here, but we will look at the practical, insightful wisdom Pope Francis offers on the issue of unresolved anger and its effect on the family:

> My advice is never to let the day end without making peace in the family. "And how am I going to make peace? By getting down on my knees? No! Just by a small gesture, a little something, and harmony within your family will be restored. Just a little caress, no words are necessary. But do not let the day end without making peace in your family." Our first reaction when we are annoyed should be one of heartfelt blessing, asking God to bless, free and heal that person.[420]

And:

> When we have been offended or let down, forgiveness is possible and desirable, but no one can say that it is easy. The truth is that "family communion can only be preserved and perfected through a great spirit of sacrifice. It requires, in fact, a ready and generous openness of each and all to understanding, to forbearance, to pardon,

to reconciliation. There is no family that does not know how selfishness, discord, tension and conflict violently attack and at times mortally wound its own communion: hence there arise the many and varied forms of division in family life."[421]

The chapter concludes with a wonderful reflection on the "transformation of love." Over time, married couples face inevitable changes to their relationship:

In the course of every marriage physical appearances change, but this hardly means that love and attraction need fade. We love the other person for who they are, not simply for their body. Although the body ages, it still expresses that personal identity that first won our heart. Even if others can no longer see the beauty of that identity, a spouse continues to see it with the eyes of love and so his or her affection does not diminish. He or she reaffirms the decision to belong to the other and expresses that choice in faithful and loving closeness. The nobility of this decision, by its intensity and depth, gives rise to a new kind of emotion as they fulfill their marital mission. For "emotion, caused by another human being as a person ... does not per se tend toward the conjugal act." It finds other sensible expressions. Indeed, love "is a single reality, but with different dimensions; at different times, one or other dimension may emerge more clearly." The marriage bond finds new forms of expression and constantly seeks new ways to grow in strength. These both preserve and strengthen the bond. They call for daily effort. None of this, however, is possible without praying to the Holy Spirit for an outpouring of his grace, his supernatural strength and his spiritual fire, to confirm, direct and transform our love in every new situation.[422]

Love Made Fruitful

Chapter Five focuses on love's fruitfulness (procreation), a topic we have seen covered in depth in previous papal documents. This document speaks in a deeply spiritual and psychological manner about welcoming new life, the waiting period of pregnancy, and the love between mother and father,[423] as well as the gift of adoption.

Rather than speak of the "nuclear" family, *Amoris* encourages us to think of families in the broad sense, which includes aunts and uncles, cousins, friends, and relatives of friends. The family is a wide network of many relationships, and the Sacrament of Matrimony has a deeply social character.

Within this spiritual dimension, the relationship between youths and the elderly, as well as the relationship between brothers and sisters, is a training ground for relating with others:

> This larger family should provide love and support to teenage mothers, children without parents, single mothers left to raise children, persons with disabilities needing particular affection and closeness, young people struggling with addiction, the unmarried, separated or widowed who are alone, and the elderly and infirm who lack the support of their children. It should also embrace "even those who have made a shipwreck of their lives." This wider family can help make up for the shortcomings of parents, detect and report possible situations in which children suffer violence and even abuse, and provide wholesome love and family stability in cases when parents prove incapable of this.[424]

Some Pastoral Perspectives

Chapter Six responds to various discussions during both the 2014 and 2015 synods regarding the need for new pastoral programs aimed at evangelizing the family. In general, families should not only be evangelized, they also need to evangelize. This must be developed at the local level, as "different communities will have to devise more practical and effective initiatives that respect both the Church's teaching and local problems and needs."[425]

It is also important to look at the more significant pastoral challenges facing the Church today. Pope Francis recognizes that many priests, deacons, men and women religious, catechists, and other pastoral workers often lack the training needed to deal with the complex problems currently facing families. Seminarians could also benefit from better formation:

> Seminarians should receive a more extensive interdisciplinary, and not merely doctrinal, formation in the areas of engagement and marriage. Their training does not always allow them to explore their own psychological and affective background and experiences. Some come from troubled families, with absent parents and a lack of emotional stability. There is a need to ensure that the formation process can enable them to attain the maturity and psychological balance needed for their future ministry. Family bonds are essential for reinforcing healthy self-esteem. It is important for families to be part of the seminary process and priestly life, since they help to reaffirm these and to keep them well grounded in reality. It is helpful for seminarians to combine time in the seminary with time spent in parishes.[426]

Following this, there is also a need for improved marriage

preparation for engaged couples, including accompaniment of these couples in the first years of married life. Crises are inevitable, sure to touch every family, yet "each crisis has a lesson to teach us; we need to learn how to listen for it with the ear of the heart":[427]

> The life of every family is marked by all kinds of crises, yet these are also part of its dramatic beauty. Couples should be helped to realize that surmounting a crisis need not weaken their relationship; instead, it can improve, settle and mature the wine of their union. Life together should not diminish but increase their contentment; every new step along the way can help couples find new ways to happiness. Each crisis becomes an apprenticeship in growing closer together or learning a little more about what it means to be married. There is no need for couples to resign themselves to an inevitable downward spiral or a tolerable mediocrity. On the contrary, when marriage is seen as a challenge that involves overcoming obstacles, each crisis becomes an opportunity to let the wine of their relationship age and improve. Couples will gain from receiving help in facing crises, meeting challenges and acknowledging them as part of family life. Experienced and trained couples should be open to offering guidance, so the couples will not be unnerved by these crises or tempted to hasty decisions.[428]

Good communication is critical, particularly in times of crisis:

> Crises need to be faced together. This is hard, since persons sometimes withdraw in order to avoid saying what they feel; they retreat into a craven silence.

At these times, it becomes all the more important to create opportunities for speaking heart to heart. Unless a couple learns to do this, they will find it harder and harder as time passes. Communication is an art learned in moments of peace in order to be practiced in moments of difficulty. Spouses need help in discovering their deepest thoughts and feelings and expressing them. Like childbirth, this is a painful process that brings forth a new treasure.[429]

In this same line of thinking, it's important to accompany abandoned, separated, and divorced persons. Too often, the "slowness of the [annulment] process causes distress and strain on the parties,"[430] which is why Pope Francis has worked to speed up the process for people to receive declarations nullity.[431]

We also cannot forget the suffering of children in situations of conflict: "Divorce is an evil, and the increasing number of divorces is very troubling. Hence, our most important pastoral task with regard to families is to strengthen their love, helping to heal wounds and working to prevent the spread of this drama of our times."[432]

Regarding families with members with homosexual tendencies, we must respect them and refrain from any unjust discrimination and every form of aggression or violence. At the same time, the exhortation clearly rejects the notion of same-sex marriage:

"As for proposals to place unions between homosexual persons on the same level as marriage, there are absolutely no grounds for considering homosexual unions to be in any way similar or even remotely analogous to God's plan for marriage and family." It is unacceptable "that local Churches should be subjected to pressure in this matter and that international bodies should make financial aid to poor countries dependent on the introduction of laws to establish 'marriage' between persons of the same sex."[433]

This has always been the teaching of the Church, so nothing is different here. However, Francis stresses that Christians should be "content to leave judgment to God, determined to walk alongside those who struggle, trusting always in the merciful judgment of God."[434]

Toward a Better Education of Children

Chapter Seven is dedicated to the human, intellectual, and spiritual formation of children. Parents are the child's first educators, and they exercise the most influence over the moral development of their children. For this reason, families today are encouraged to "rethink their methods and discover new resources":[435]

> Parents need to consider what they want their children to be exposed to, and this necessarily means being concerned about who is providing their entertainment, who is entering their rooms through television and electronic devices, and with whom they are spending their free time. Only if we devote time to our children, speaking of important things with simplicity and concern, and finding healthy ways for them to spend their time, will we be able to shield them from harm. Vigilance is always necessary and neglect is never beneficial. Parents have to help prepare children and adolescents to confront the risk, for example, of aggression, abuse or drug addiction.[436]

At the same time, obsession is not education:

> We cannot control every situation that a child may

experience. Here it remains true that "time is greater than space." In other words, it is more important
to start processes than to dominate spaces. If parents are obsessed with always knowing where their
children are and controlling all their movements,
they will seek only to dominate space. But this is no
way to educate, strengthen and prepare their children to face challenges. What is most important is
the ability lovingly to help them grow in freedom,
maturity, overall discipline, and real autonomy....
The real question, then, is not where our children
are physically, or whom they are with at any given
time, but rather where they are existentially, where
they stand in terms of their convictions, goals, desires and dreams. The questions I would put to parents are these: "Do we seek to understand 'where'
our children really are in their journey? Where is
their soul, do we really know? And above all, do we
want to know?"[437]

This chapter also discusses the need for appropriate sex education:

Frequently, sex education deals primarily with
"protection" through the practice of "safe sex."
Such expressions convey a negative attitude towards the natural procreative finality of sexuality, as
if an eventual child were an enemy to be protected
against. This way of thinking promotes narcissism
and aggressivity in place of acceptance. It is always
irresponsible to invite adolescents to toy with their
bodies and their desires, as if they possessed the
maturity, values, mutual commitment and goals
proper to marriage. They end up being blithely en-

couraged to use other persons as a means of fulfilling their needs or limitations. The important thing is to teach them sensitivity to different expressions of love, mutual concern and care, loving respect and deeply meaningful communication. All of these prepare them for an integral and generous gift of self that will be expressed, following a public commitment, in the gift of their bodies. Sexual union in marriage will thus appear as a sign of an all-inclusive commitment, enriched by everything that has preceded it.[438]

Accompanying, Discerning and Integrating Weakness

Chapter Eight deals with people's personal circumstances. It is a sensitive chapter, and "an isolated reading of Chapter Eight that interprets the text out of its context is of no help whatsoever."[439] It grapples with issues such as cohabitation, divorce, and civil unions, which have no easy solutions:

> The Synod Fathers stated that, although the Church realizes that any breach of the marriage bond "is against the will of God," she is also "conscious of the frailty of many of her children." Illumined by the gaze of Jesus Christ, "she turns with love to those who participate in her life in an incomplete manner, recognizing that the grace of God works also in their lives by giving them the courage to do good, to care for one another in love and to be of service to the community in which they live and work."... Although she constantly holds up the call to perfection and asks for a fuller response to God, "the Church must accompany with attention and care the weakest of her children, who show signs of a wounded and troubled love, by restoring in them

> hope and confidence, like the beacon of a light-
> house in a port or a torch carried among the people
> to enlighten those who have lost their way or who
> are in the midst of a storm." Let us not forget that
> the Church's task is often like that of a field hospi-
> tal.[440]

It is important to remember that this document, and particularly Chapter Eight, follows the recommendations[441] of the synod
fathers. Recall also that Francis has already stated that this exhortation presents no doctrinal or disciplinary changes, since answers
do not always have to be sought along these lines.[442] So, in con-
junction with the synod, "the document states that *love* — that is
love between a man and a woman, love until death and open to
life, despite everything — is the source of all possible progress."[443]

Consequently, this chapter is an invitation to mercy and pastoral discernment in situations that do not fully match what the
Lord proposes. By way of example, Pope Francis is particularly
concerned that "many young people today distrust marriage and
live together, putting off indefinitely the commitment of marriage,
while yet others break a commitment already made and immediately assume a new one."[444]

Concerning the issue of divorced and remarried Catholics, the
"divorced who have entered a new union, for example, can find
themselves in a variety of situations, which should not be pigeon-
holed or fit into overly rigid classifications leaving no room for
a suitable personal and pastoral discernment."[445] Moreover, "the
baptized who are divorced and civilly remarried need to be more
fully integrated into Christian communities in the variety of ways
possible, while avoiding any occasion of scandal."[446]

For situations such as these, we use three important verbs: *accompanying*, *discerning*, and *integrating*, in that order. All of these
steps are fundamental for addressing "fragile, complex or irregular
situations."[447] No matter the circumstance, "all these situations re-

quire a constructive response seeking to transform them into opportunities that can lead to the fullness of marriage and family in
conformity with the Gospel. These couples need to be welcomed
and guided patiently and discreetly."[448]

Accompanying is the initial approach that the Church "makes
with her children to establish a stable, ongoing, rapport."[449] In
contrast to offering a hurried solution to their problems, to accompany someone on their walk to truth, there must be an awareness that time is needed for "the truth of love to mature in the
person."[450]

Pastoral *discernment* is the next step on the journey. Assuming that the goal is full communion with the Catholic Church (in
order to receive the Eucharist), many people have to go through
a period of discernment, during which they may have to face the
reality that there are impediments for them to overcome. The goal
of discernment, then, is not to find a way to admit everyone to
holy Communion. The purpose of discernment is also not to get
around Church norms or discover gaps in the law so as to satisfy
everyone and to give them what they want.[451] Instead:

> Discernment consists in helping individuals to be-
> come aware of their situation in God's sight, in order
> to participate more fully in the life of the Church
> and to respond to God's will with sincerity, humili-
> ty, and in conformity with the requirements of truth
> and charity. For them, this in turn will mean go-
> ing back to living according to the truth of their
> marriage bond. Indeed, what Francis wishes for the
> Church is precisely "pastoral care ... centered on
> the marriage bond," which contrasts with the "cul-
> ture of the ephemeral" that he often denounces.[452]

There are three main criteria for those in irregular situations,
which must be met for total integration into the Catholic Church:

"professing and living out the faith of the Church; being in communion with the body of the Church, through her pastors; and leading a life that is in harmony with the sacraments."[453] The last point is precisely the one where the main difficulty appears. Frequently, lack of consistency with the sacramental life influences the first aspect, the life of faith. This explains why the pope insists that there be adequate time and effort for accompaniment and discernment, as *these things take time.*

Once again, Pope Francis is not talking about changing theology or Church law relative to marriage. He is also not encouraging individual priests to let divorced and remarried (without an annulment) Catholics come to Communion whenever they like. Rather, he is reminding us that divorced and remarried Catholics are not excommunicated:

> It is important that the divorced who have entered a new union should be made to feel part of the Church. "They are not excommunicated" and they should not be treated as such, since they remain part of the ecclesial community. These situations "require careful discernment and respectful accompaniment. Language or conduct that might lead them to feel discriminated against should be avoided, and they should be encouraged to participate in the life of the community. The Christian community's care of such persons is not to be considered a weakening of its faith and testimony to the indissolubility of marriage; rather, such care is a particular expression of its charity."[454]

The novelty of Chapter Eight is that it shows Francis' merciful approach, his desire to bring the Gospel to those who are far off, following a logical progression of integration. *Amoris Laetitia* announces the Gospel of the Family, inviting everyone to take part, in whatever situation they may find themselves. Pope Francis is saying, "Let us make this journey as families, let us keep walking together."[455]

The Spirituality of Marriage and Family

The final chapter is relatively short, presenting a spirituality of marriage and family life that might well renew the world. It is now up to couples, children, and the Church to foster a culture of nuptial love, a love that humanizes the world, which has forgotten how to love unconditionally. In essence, "Marriage, family life: this is how to deal with a throwaway culture, a culture of disrespect, a culture of a heart grown cold."[456] If the New Evangelization is actually going to come into existence, it will be through marriage and the family.

Chapter Eight Reflection Questions

Where were you when you heard that Jorge Bergoglio was the new pope, Pope Francis? What was your first impression of him?

What is your opinion of having not only a top-down, but also a horizontal, Church? What are some issues that might be better handled by the local Church rather than the magisterium?

Although he has never said this, there are those who believe that the Catholic Church, through Pope Francis, is trying to make peace with the sexual revolution. Is there any way to make this happen?

Pope Francis reasons that the family is a wide network of many relationships, claiming that the Sacrament of Matrimony has a deeply social character. How might your life be different if you treated your whole network of family, friends, and acquaintances as if they were your nuclear family?

Pope Francis touched on the need for appropriate sex education for children and adolescents today. This would include preparing them (when the time is right) to understand what it means to make an integral and generous gift of self, to be aware of their own bodies, to be sensitive to different expressions of love, etc. What are different ways to do this, and at what age should this be done?

Pope Francis encourages us to reach out to those who are in imperfect or irregular situations to help bring them back into full communion in the Church. How might you reach out to a young couple who is cohabitating, but still attends Sunday Mass? Or a divorced person, who is remarried outside of the Church, but still wants to participate in the life of the parish?

NOTES

1   Andrea Gagliarducci, "Why the drafting of 'Humanae Vitae' matters, 50 years later," Catholic News Agency, August 1, 2017, https://www.catholicnewsagency.com/news/why-the-drafting-of-humanae-vitae-matters-50-years-later-64907.

2   George Weigel, "Lessons in Statecraft," *First Things*, May 2015, https://www.firstthings.com/article/2015/05/lessons-in-statecraft.

3   Frank Sheed, *Theology and Sanity* (San Francisco: Ignatius Press, 1978), 22.

4   Romano Guardini, quote in Henri de Lubac, *The Splendor of the Church*, 2nd ed.(San Francisco: Ignatius Press, 1999), 184.

5   There are several levels of papal teaching. Not all teaching documents that come from the pope carry the same weight or require the same personal adherence from the faithful. Encyclicals are the most important papal letters, and they are addressed to the entire Church on some matter of particular importance. Encyclicals should be read with the intention of full obedience.

6   Pope John Paul II, *Veritatis Splendor* ("The Splendor of Truth"), August 6, 1993, http://w2.vatican.va/content/john-paul-ii/en/encyclicals/documents/hf_jp-ii_enc_06081993_veritatis-splendor.html, 3; *Populorum Progressio* and *Gaudium et Spes* are original sources.

7   W. Bradford Wilcox, "The Evolution of Divorce," *National Affairs* 32 (Summer 2017), https://www.nationalaffairs.com/publications/detail/the-evolution-of-divorce.

8   Pope John Paul II, *Familiaris Consortio* (on the role of the Christian family in the modern world), November 22, 1981, http://w2.vatican.va/content/john-paul-ii/en/apost_exhortations/documents/hf_jp-ii_exh_19811122_familiaris-consortio.html.

9   Pope Benedict XVI, *Deus Caritas Est* ("God Is Love"), November 25, 2005, http://w2.vatican.va/content/benedict-xvi/en/encyclicals/documents/hf_ben-xvi_enc_20051225_deus-caritas-est.html.

10   Gagliarducci, "Why the drafting of 'Humanae Vitae' matters."

11   Ibid.

12   See Warren H. Carroll and Anne W. Carroll, *The Crisis of Christendom*, Vol. 6 (Front Royal, VA: Christendom Press, 2013), 373–374.

13   See Msgr. Charles Pope, "There was something about the 20th century, something awful. Did Pope Leo XIII have the answer?" March 29, 2002, http://blog.adw.org/2012/03/there-is-something-about-the-20th-century-something-awful-did-pope-leo-have-the-answer/. This story is part of Catholic tradition and it can be found in numerous books and articles regarding Pope Leo XIII.

14   Ibid.

15   Carroll, *The Crisis of Christendom*, Vol. 6, 221.

16   Father Paul Pearson, "What is Catholic Social Teaching?", accessed October 15, 2017, https://www.catholicculture.org/culture/library/view.cfm?recnum=7732.

17   He was forced to migrate to the Belgian capital in 1845 after being expelled from both Germany and France because of the political ideology he was spreading.

18   At that time, the words "socialism" and "communism" were used somewhat interchangeably. Engels noted that when it was written, they could not call it a *Socialist* manifesto because a number of other sects throughout Europe were calling themselves socialists. Also, communism was a working-class movement, while socialism was a middle-class movement. Since the *Manifesto* addressed the needs of the working class, it had to be called *The Communist Manifesto*. Of all the documents written by Karl Marx, it is still one of the most widely read and is still very popular. It is worth noting that late in his life, Engels explained that while this was a collaborative project, the ideas belonged to Marx.

19   Karl Marx, *The Communist Manifesto*.

20   Ibid.

21   Pope Leo XIII, *Quod Apostolici Muneris* (on socialism), December 28, 1878, http://w2.vatican.va/content/leo-xiii/en/encyclicals/documents/hf_l-xiii_enc_28121878_quod-apostolici-muneris.html, 1.

22   Ibid., 8.

23   Ibid.

24   David Deavel, "The Catholic Church and the Seven Deadly Sins

of Socialism," June 2, 2016, https://stream.org/catholic-church-seven-deadly-sins-socialism/.

25   Pontifical Council for Justice and Peace (under Pope John Paul II), *Compendium of the Social Doctrine of the Church* (Washington, DC: USCCB Publishing, 2005), 214.

26   Peter A. Kwasniewski, "Forgotten Treasures — The Counterrevolutionary Lion," *Lay Witness*, January/February 2008.

27   J. E. Copius, S.J., "The Personality of Pope Leo XIII: An Appreciation," *The World To-Day*, August 1903.

28   Ibid.

29   See Pope Leo XIII, *Arcanum*, May 10, 1880, http://w2.vatican.va/content/leo-xiii/en/encyclicals/documents/hf_l-xiii_enc_10021880_arcanum.html, 28.

30   "Arcanum," New Advent Catholic Encyclopedia, Kevin Knight, ed., accessed October 15, 2017, http://www.newadvent.org/cathen/01687e.htm.

31   Anthony Esolen, "Healthy Societies Need Successful Marriages," *Crisis* magazine, December 19, 2012, http://www.crisismagazine.com/2012/healthy-societies-require-successful-marriages.

32   Mary Shivanandan, *Crossing the Threshold of Hope: A New Vision of Marriage in the Light of John Paul II's Anthropology* (Washington, DC: The Catholic University of America Press, 1999), 192.

33   Leo XIII, *Arcanum*, 5.

34   Ibid., emphasis added.

35   See "Arcanum" at New Advent Catholic Encyclopedia.

36   *Arcanum*, 6.

37   Ibid., 1.

38   Ibid., 2.

39   Ibid., 9.

40   Ibid.

41   Ibid., 11.

42   Ibid., 12; see also Eph 6:4.

43   Ibid., 26.

44   Ibid., 10.

45   Andrew M. Greenwell, "Natural Law of Marriage: *Arcanum divinae sapientia*," Lex Christianorum, February 8, 2001, http://lexchristianorum.blogspot.com/2011/02/natural-law-of-marriage-arcanum-divinae.html. Serial polygamy is having more than one wife/husband, not just one at a time.

46   *Arcanum*, 30.

47   Ibid., 29.

48   Ibid.

49   Ibid., 44.

50   Ibid., 42.

51   *CCC* 2096.

52   *Arcanum*, 41.

53   See "Arcanum" at New Advent Catholic Encyclopedia.

54   *Arcanum*, 26.

55   Ibid., 43.

56   Anthony Esolen, *Defending Marriage: Twelve Arguments for Sanity* (Charlotte, NC: Saint Benedict Press, 2014), Kindle edition.

57   Pope Francis, *The Church of Mercy* (Chicago: Loyola Press, 2014), Kindle edition.

58   See Harold Tribble Cole, *The Coming Terror* (New York: Languine, 1936), 23.

59   Allan Carlson, "Sanger's Victory: How Planned Parenthood's Founder Played the Christians and Won," *Touchstone* magazine, accessed December 8, 2015, http://www.touchstonemag.com/archives/article.php?id=24-01-039-f.

60   Thomas R. Ascik, "'Only Yesterday,' today, and the decline of religion," *Catholic World Report*, January 2, 2018, http://www.catholicworldreport.com/2018/01/02/only-yesterday-today-and-the-decline-of-religion/.

61   Frederick Lewis Allen, *Only Yesterday: An Informal History of the 1920s* (New York: Open Road Integrated Media, originally published in 1931, reprinted in 2010), Kindle edition.

62   Ascik, "Only Yesterday,' today, and the decline of religion."

63   See John F. Kippley, "*Casti Connubii*: 60 Years Later, More Relevant Than Ever," *Homiletic and Pastoral Review*, June 1991, https://www.ewtn.com/library/MARRIAGE/CASTI.TXT.

64   Shivanandan, *Crossing the Threshold of Hope: A New Vision of Marriage*, 195.

65   Ibid.

66   Ibid., 183.

67   Angela Franks, "The Gift of Female Fertility: Church Teaching on Contraception," in *Women, Sex, and the Church*, Erika Bachiochi, ed. (Pauline Books & Media, 2010), 100.

68   Carlson, "Sanger's Victory: How Planned Parenthood's Founder Played the Christians and Won."

69   Ibid.

70   See Kevin D. Williamson, "Planned Parenthood's Century of Brutality," *National Review*, June 19, 2017, http://www.nationalreview.com/article/448746/planned-parenthoods-brutal-century.

71   See Kippley, "*Casti Connubii*: 60 Years Later, More Relevant Than Ever."

72   Carlson, "Sanger's Victory: How Planned Parenthood's Founder Played the Christians and Won."

73   Catholic Answers, "Birth Control," accessed December 8, 2017, https://www.catholic.com/tract/birth-control.

74   Every ten years since 1867, at the invitation of the archbishop of Canterbury, the Anglican bishops from all over the world are invited to gather together to discuss issues pertaining to the Church. The conference gets its name from Lambeth Palace, the archbishop of Canterbury's residence in London, where the conference used to be held.

75   Resolution 15 of the 1930 Lambeth Conference, recounted by John S. Hamlon, "From Lambeth to the Land of Nod," in *Catholic World Report*, May 22, 2015, http://www.catholicworldreport.com/2015/05/22/from-lambeth-to-the-land-of-nod/, emphasis added.

76   Resolution 68 of the 1920 Lambeth Conference.

77   Catholic Answers, "Birth Control."

78   Zsolt Aradi, *Pius XI: The Pope and the Man* (Garden City, NY: Hanover House, 1958), 6.

79   Pope Pius XI, *Casti Connubii*, December 31, 1930, https://w2.vatican.va/content/pius-xi/en/encyclicals/documents/hf_p-xi_enc_19301231_casti-connubii.html, 56.

80   George Sim Johnston, "Contraception, Conscience, and Church Authority," *The Catholic Thing*, March 21, 2015, https://www.thecatholicthing.org/2015/03/21/contraception-conscience-and-church-authority/.

81   Shivanandan, *Crossing the Threshold of Hope: A New Vision of Marriage*, 190.

82   See Ibid.

83   Pius XI, *Casti Connubii*, 6.

84   See Walter J. Handren, S.J., *No Longer Two: A Commentary on the Encyclical Casti Connubii of Pius XI* (Westminster, MD: The Newman Press, 1955), 27.

85   Leila M. Lawler, *"God Has No Grandchildren: A Guided Reading of Pope Pius XI Encyclical Casti Connubii, On Chaste Marriage"* (Amazon Digital Services), Kindle edition.

86   *Casti Connubii*, 6.

87   Handren, *No Longer Two*, 31.

88   *Casti Connubii*, 7.

89   Ibid., 11.

90   Ibid., 16.

91   Ibid., 84.

92   Handren, *No Longer Two*, 51.

93   *Casti Connubii*, 23.

94   Ibid.

95   Handren, *No Longer Two*, 72.

96   See Ibid.

97   *Casti Connubii*, 40.

98   Handren, *No Longer Two*, 104.

99   *Casti Connubii*, 53.

100   Ibid., 54.

101   Margaret Sanger, "Birth Control Advances: A Reply to the Pope" January 13, 1931, https://www.nyu.edu/projects/sanger/webedition/app/documents/show.php?sangerDoc=236637.xml.

102   Handren, *No Longer Two*, 139.

103   Ibid., 221.

104   The Editors, "Pope Paul VI: 1963–1978," *America* magazine, November 5, 2014, https://www.americamagazine.org/issue/pope-paul-vi-1963-1978. Reprinted from a 1978 article. Emphasis added.

105   Ibid.

106   See George Weigel, *Witness to Hope: The Biography of Pope John Paul II* (New York: HarperCollins Publishers, Ltd., 2011), Kindle edition.

107   Russell Shaw, "This year marks the 50th anniversary of Vatican II — here's a look at why it rocked the Church," OSV Newsweekly, August 15, 2012, https://www.osv.com/TheChurch/Jesus/Article/TabId/739/ArtMID/13697/ArticleID/8571/Second-Vatican-Council.aspx.

108   Douglas Bushman, "The True Spirit of Vatican II," *The Catholic World Report*, December 2, 2012, http://www.catholicworldreport.com/2012/12/02/the-true-spirit-of-vatican-ii/.

109   See Ibid.

110   Ibid.

111   Ibid.

112   See Ibid.

113   Weigel, *Witness to Hope*.

114   Ibid.

115   Ibid.

116   Joseph Pronechen. "John XXIII and the Real Second Vatican Council," *National Catholic Register*, April 25, 2014, http://www.ncregister.com/site/article/john-xxiii-and-the-real-second-vatican-council.

117   Ibid.

118   Ibid.

119   See Ibid.

120   Ibid.

121   Ibid.

122   See William Doino Jr., "Rediscovering Paul VI," *First Things*, December 31, 2012, https://www.firstthings.com/web-exclusives/2012/12/rediscovering-paul-vi.

123   Ibid.

124   Ibid.

125   See Pope Paul VI, *Ecclesiam Suam* (on the Church), August 6, 1964, http://w2.vatican.va/content/paul-vi/en/encyclicals/documents/hf_p-vi_enc_06081964_ecclesiam.html. Paul dedicated a portion of this encyclical to the importance of dialogue.

126   Edward B. Fiske, "The Reign of Pope Paul: A Bridge Between Eras," *The New York Times*, August 7, 1978, http://www.nytimes.com/1978/08/07/archives/the-reign-of-pope-paul-a-bridge-between-eras-creative-initial-years.html.

127   Russell Shaw, "Pope Paul VI gets his due," OSV Daily Take, September 29, 2014, https://www.osv.com/OSVNewsweekly/National/Article/TabId/717/ArtMID/13622/ArticleID/16154/Pope-Paul-VI-gets-his-due.aspx.

128   Andrea Tornielli, "Paul VI: The Pope of Suffering Humanity," *Vatican Insider*, April 26, 2011, http://www.lastampa.it/2011/04/26/vaticaninsider/eng/the-vatican/paul-vi-the-pope-of-suffering-humanity-bG8Z7byDWFf4IAvgzeBsjO/pagina.html.

129   "Margaret Sanger," accessed January 20, 2018, https://legacyofmargaretsanger.weebly.com/.

130   Weigel, *Witness to Hope*.

131   Father Peter Ryan, S.J., "*Humanae Vitae* in Historical and Social Perspective," YouTube video filmed at Franciscan University of Steubenville, based on an unpublished paper by the same name, with Father Ryan's permission.

132   See Ibid.

133   Ibid.

134   Ibid.

135   See Weigel, *Witness to Hope.*

136   Father Peter Ryan, S.J., "*Humanae Vitae* in Historical and Social Perspective"

137   Ryan, "*Humanae Vitae* in Historical and Social Perspective"; also see Russell Shaw, "Watershed Moment," July 27, 2008, http://www.osv.com/TheChurch/ChurchDocuments/PapalDocuments/Article/TabId/1333/ArtMID/15273/ArticleID/10236/Watershed-Moment.aspx.

138   Ryan, "*Humanae Vitae* in Historical and Social Perspective."

139   Doino Jr., "Rediscovering Paul VI."

140   Tornielli, "Paul VI: The Pope of Suffering Humanity."

141   See Shivanandan, *Crossing the Threshold of Hope: A New Vision of Marriage,* 190.

142   Ralph M. McInerny, *What Went Wrong with Vatican II: The Catholic Crisis Explained* (Manchester, NH: Sophia Institute Press, 1998), 102.

143   Pope Paul VI, *Humanae Vitae,* July 25, 1968, http://w2.vatican.va/content/paul-vi/en/encyclicals/documents/hf_p-vi_enc_25071968_humanae-vitae.html, 1. [Hereafter *HV.*]

144   Ibid.

145   *HV,* 2. Pope Paul uses the word "man" in a generic sense, meaning both men and women.

146   *HV,* 4.

147   See *CCC* 1957.

148   Ibid., 1958.

149   *HV,* 4.

150   Ibid., 7.

151   Ibid.

152   Ibid., 9.

153   Ibid., 10.

154   Ibid.

155   Ibid., 17.

156   *CCC* 2377.

157   See Doino Jr., "Rediscovering Paul VI."

158   Joseph McAuley, "An Isaiah Pope: Paul VI," *America* magazine, October 17, 2014, https://www.americamagazine.org/content/all-things/isaiah-pope-paul-vi.

159   A Synod of Bishops is a meeting of bishops from all over the world who gather to discuss various doctrinal or pastoral matters. The bishops are referred to as synod fathers. They are expected to offer suggestions to the pope, which may or may not become official Church teaching.

160   Thomas Reese, "Looking back at the 1980 synod on the family," National Catholic Reporter, September 12, 2014, https://www.ncronline.org/blogs/faith-and-justice/looking-back-1980-synod-family.

161   Weigel, *Witness to Hope,* Kindle edition.

162   Ibid.

163   Ibid.

164   Apostolic exhortations are commonly issued in response to an assembly of the Synod of Bishops, in which case they are known as post-synodal apostolic exhortations.

165   Dr. William Newton, "The Legacy of the Vision of Pope John Paul II for Marriage and Family," *Homiletic and Pastoral Review*, November 14, 2014, http://www.hprweb.com/2014/11/the-legacy-of-the-vision-of-pope-john-paul-ii-for-marriage-and-family/.

166   See Ibid.

167   Mary Eberstadt, "The Prophetic Power of *Humanae Vitae,*" *First Things*, April 2018, https://www.firstthings.com/article/2018/04/the-prophetic-power-of-humanae-vitae.

168   Newton, "The Legacy of the Vision of Pope John Paul II for Marriage and Family."

169   Ibid.

170   See Weigel, *Witness to Hope*, Kindle edition.

171   Newton, "The Legacy of the Vision of Pope John Paul II for Marriage and Family."

172   Pope John Paul II, *Letter to Families* (*Gratissimam Sane*), February 2, 1994, https://w2.vatican.va/content/john-paul-ii/en/letters/1994/documents/hf_jp-ii_let_02021994_families.html, 23.

173   Cardinal Carlo Caffarra was archbishop emeritus of Bologna, Italy, and founding president of the Pontifical John Paul II Institute for Studies on

Marriage and Family.

174   Edward Pentin, "Cardinal Caffarra: Satan is Hurling at God the 'Ultimate and Terrible Challenge,'" *National Catholic Register,* May 20, 2017, http://www.ncregister.com/blog/edward-pentin/cardinal-caffarra-satan-is-hurling-at-god-the-ultimate-and-terrible-challen.

175   Ibid.

176   Ibid.

177   Ibid.

178   Ibid.

179   Ibid.

180   Edward Pentin, "Why Education Is Key to Protecting Life, Marriage and the Family" in the *National Catholic Register*, May 30, 2017, http://www.ncregister.com/daily-news/why-education-is-key-to-protecting-life-marriage-and-the-family.

181   On September 19, 2017, Pope Francis established a new John Paul II Pontifical Theological Institute for Marriage and Family Sciences to replace the previous academic institution founded by John Paul in 1981.

182   Sister Lucia died in 2005 at the age of ninety-seven, at the Carmelite convent of Santa Teresa in Coimbra, Portugal, where she had lived since 1948. At ten years old, she was the oldest of the three shepherd children who witnessed apparitions of the Blessed Virgin Mary from May to October 1917. The other two were her cousins Francisco and Jacinta Marto, who were just nine and seven, respectively. Francisco and Jacinta both died in childhood and were canonized on May 13, 2017, the hundredth anniversary of the apparitions.

183   Joseph Pronechen, "Fatima: Sr. Lucia and John Paul II: Why Every Family Should Be a Holy Family," National Catholic Regiser, December 31, 2017, http://www.ncregister.com/blog/joseph-pronechen/sister-lucia-and-st-john-paul-ii-explain-holy-families-for-holy-family-sund, emphasis added.

184   Angelus address, May 29, 1994, http://w2.vatican.va/content/john-paul-ii/it/angelus/1994/documents/hf_jp-ii_ang_19940529.html, translated from the Italian.

185   Ibid.

186   Newton, "The Legacy of the Vision of Pope John Paul II for Marriage

and Family."

187   John Paul II, *Crossing the Threshold of Hope* (New York: Alfred A. Knopf, 1994), 122.

188   Ibid., 123.

189   Pope John Paul II's given name was Karol Wojtyla.

190   Newton, "The Legacy of the Vision of Pope John Paul II for Marriage and Family."

191   John Paul II, *Familiaris Consortio.* [Hereafter *FC*.]

192   Ibid., 6.

193   John S. Hamlon, *A Call to Families: Study Guide and Commentary for* Familiaris Consortio (Collegeville, MN: Human Life Center, 1984), 7.

194   Ibid., 8.

195   *FC*, 8, quoting Second Vatican Council *Gaudium et Spes* (Pastoral Constitution on the Church in the Modern World), December 7, 1965,   http://www.vatican.va/archive/hist_councils/ii_vatican_council/documents/vat-ii_const_19651207_gaudium-et-spes_en.html, 15.

196   Ibid.

197   Newton, "The Legacy of the Vision of Pope John Paul II for Marriage and Family."

198   Hamlon, *A Call to Families*, 18.

199   Ibid.

200   *FC*, 14.

201   Ibid.

202   Ibid., 17.

203   Hamlon, *A Call to Families*, 27.

204   Ibid., 29.

205   *FC*, 21.

206   Ibid., 25.

207   Ibid., 26.

208   Ibid., 27.

209   Ibid., 33.

210   Ibid., 37.

211   Ibid., 75.

212   Weigel, *Witness to Hope*.

213   Gregory R. Beabout, "What is the legacy of Pope John Paul II?" Acton Institute, April 13, 2005, https://acton.org/node/3620.

214   See Ibid.

215   Ibid.

216   R. Jared Staudt, "Culture in the Magisterium of Pope John Paul II: Evangelization through Dialogue and the Renewal of Society," *Claritas: Journal of Dialogue and Culture*, vol. 3, no. 1 (March 2014), 52–65.

217   Beabout, "What is the legacy of Pope John Paul II?"

218   Staudt, "Culture in the Magisterium of Pope John Paul II." Original citation is Pope John Paul II, Address to UNESCO, "Man's Entire Humanity is Expressed in Culture," June 2, 1980, 14.

219   George Weigel, *The Cube and the Cathedral: Europe, America, and Politics without God* (New York: Basic Books, 2006), 30.

220   Staudt, "Culture in the Magisterium of Pope John Paul II."

221   Ibid.

222   Beabout, "What is the legacy of Pope John Paul II?"

223   Staudt, "Culture in the Magisterium of Pope John Paul II."

224   Ibid.

225   The word "sects" has to do with the new religious movements. A further explanation can be found on the EWTN website: https://www.ewtn .com/library/NEWAGE/ARINNEWM.TXT. There you will find a copy of Cardinal Francis Arinze's address at the April 4–7, 1991, consistory at the Vatican. His presentation is called "The Challenge of New Movements," and his reflections include such things as: terminology; typology of the new religious movements; origin of the new religious movements and reasons for their spread; problems posed by the new religious movements; pastoral response, general; pastoral response, specific.

226   Weigel, *Witness to Hope*.

227   George Weigel, quoted in *National Catholic Register*, "A 'Culture of Life' or a 'Tyrant State'?" by Joan Frawley Desmond, March 28, 2015, http:// www.ncregister.com/daily-news/evangelium-vitae-turns-20.

228   Pope John Paul II, *Evangelium Vitae* ("The Gospel of Life"), March 25, 1995, http://w2.vatican.va/content/john-paul-ii/en/encyclicals/documents/hf_jp-ii_enc_25031995_evangelium-vitae.html, 64. [Hereafter *EV.*]

229   Ibid.

230   Ibid.

231   Beabout, "What is the legacy of Pope John Paul II?"

232   See Kenneth Woodward, "Life, Death, and The Pope," *Newsweek*, April 9, 1995, http://www.newsweek.com/life-death-and-pope-181514.

233   Weigel, *Witness to Hope.*

234   *EV,* see 20.

235   Ibid., 18; also see Joan Frawley Desmond, "A 'Culture of Life' or a 'Tyrant State'?" March 28, 2015, *National Catholic Register*, http://www.ncregister.com/daily-news/evangelium-vitae-turns-20.

236   *EV*, 9.

237   Ibid., 10.

238   Ibid., 10–11.

239   Ibid., 11.

240   Ibid., 34.

241   Ibid.

242   Ibid., 47.

243   Ibid., 31.

244   Ibid., 50.

245   Ibid.

246   Ibid., 52.

247   Ibid., 57.

248   Ibid., 9.

249   Ibid., 60.

250   Ibid., 58.

251   Ibid., 62, emphasis added.

252   Ibid., 99.

253   Ibid., 56.

254   Ibid.

255   Ibid.

256   Ibid., 79.

257   Ibid., 82.

258   Ibid., 89.

259   Ibid.

260   Ibid., 101.

261   Weigel, *Witness to Hope*. Lolek was John Paul's childhood nickname.

262   Ibid.

263   Pope John Paul II, *Letter to Women*, June 29, 1995, https://w2.vatican.va/content/john-paul-ii/en/letters/1995/documents/hf_jp-ii_let_29061995_women.html, 11.

264   Ibid.

265   Congregation for the Doctrine of the Faith, *On the Collaboration of Men and Women in the Church and in the World*, May 31, 2004, http://www.vatican.va/roman_curia/congregations/cfaith/documents/rc_con_cfaith_doc_20040731_collaboration_en.html, 13.

266   After an encyclical, an apostolic letter is the second most important type of papal document. These letters have ordinary teaching authority, and, as Catholics, we are to read them with the intention of adhering to the principles put forth.

267   John Paul II, *Crossing the Threshold of Hope*, 216–217, emphasis in original.

268   John Paul II, *Letter to Women*, 2.

269   Weigel, *Witness to Hope*, emphasis in original.

270   Cardinal Stanislaw Dziwisz, *A Life with Karol: My Forty-Year Friendship with the Man Who Became Pope* (New York: Image, 2008), 167.

271   Weigel, *Witness to Hope*.

272   Together with the pope, a Synod of Bishops is a gathering of bishops who have come together to discuss a particular topic.

273   Charlotte Hays, "Preparing for the Synod on the Laity," *Crisis* magazine, February 1987, https://www.crisismagazine.com/1987/

preparing-for-the-synod-on-the-laity-4.

274   James Hitchcock, "Preparing for the Synod of the Laity," *Crisis Magazine*, February 1987, https://www.crisismagazine.com/1987/preparing-for-the-synod-on-the-laity-5.

275   Pope John Paul II, *Mulieris Dignitatem* (on the dignity and vocation of women), August 15, 1988, https://w2.vatican.va/content/john-paul-ii/en/apost_letters/1988/documents/hf_jp-ii_apl_19880815_mulieris-dignitatem.html, 1. [Hereafter *MD*.]

276   Ibid.

277   A post-synodal exhortation is commonly issued in response to a Synod of Bishops on a particular topic.

278   *MD*, 1.

279   Pope John Paul II, *Christifideles Laici* (on the vocation and the mission of the lay faithful in the Church and in the world), December 30, 2012, http://w2.vatican.va/content/john-paul-ii/en/apost_exhortations/documents/hf_jp-ii_exh_30121988_christifideles-laici.html, 49.

280   See Second Vatican Council, "Closing Speech," December 8, 1965, http://www.papalencyclicals.net/Paul06/p6closin.htm.

281   Mary Ann Glendon, *Traditions in Turmoil* (Ann Arbor, MI: Sapienta Press, 2006), 404–405.

282   *MD*, 2.

283   See Ray Flynn, Robin Moore and Jim Vrabel, *John Paul II: A Personal Portrait of the Pope and the Man* (New York: St. Martin's Griffin, 2002), Kindle edition.

284   *MD*, 1.

285   Edward Le Joly, *Mother Teresa: Messenger of God's Love* (Bandra, Mumbai: St. Pauls, 2004), 76–77.

286   Charles J. Chaput, O.F.M.Cap., *Living the Catholic Faith: Rediscovering the Basics* (Cincinnati, OH: Servant, 2001), 149.

287   Weigel, *Witness to Hope*.

288   *MD*, 3.

289   Ibid.

290   Ibid.

291   Le Joly, *Mother Teresa: Messenger of God's Love*, 75.

292   *Gaudium et Spes*, 22.

293   The Paschal Mystery is the passion, death, and resurrection of our Lord Jesus Christ. Celebrated at the Easter Triduum, the Paschal Mystery is the central mystery of the Catholic faith.

294   *MD*, 5.

295   Ibid.

296   Ibid., 6.

297   Ibid.

298   Ibid.

299   Ibid.

300   Congregation for the Doctrine of the Faith, *On the Collaboration of Men and Women in the Church and in the World*, 5.

301   *Catechism*, 356.

302   Congregation for the Doctrine of the Faith, *On the Collaboration of Men and Women in the Church and in the World*, 6.

303   Ibid.

304   *MD*, 7.

305   Ibid.

306   Ibid. (citing *Gaudium et Spes*, 24).

307   Ibid., 9.

308   Frank Sheed, *Theology and Sanity* (San Francisco: Ignatius Press, 1993), 187.

309   *MD*, 9.

310   See United States Conference of Catholic Bishops, *United States Catholic Catechism for Adults* (Washington, DC: 2006), 69.

311   Ibid.

312   Frank Sheed, *Theology and Sanity*, 193.

313   Ibid., 190.

314   *MD*, 9.

315   Mary Healy, *Men and Women are from Eden: A Study Guide to John*

Paul II's Theology of the Body (Cincinnati: Servant, 2005), 33.

316 A social-media movement that highlights sexual harassment incidents against women.

317 *MD*, 10.

318 *EV*, 99.

319 See Stephen J. Binz, *Women of the Gospels: Friends and Disciples of Jesus* (Grand Rapids, MI: Brazos Press, 2011), 1.

320 *MD*, 15.

321 Ibid., 13.

322 Ibid., 16.

323 Ibid., 17.

324 Ibid., 18.

325 Ibid.

326 *MD*, 18.

327 Ibid., 19.

328 Ibid.

329 Ibid.

330 Ibid., 20.

331 Ibid.

332 See Ibid., 24.

333 Ibid.

334 Ibid., 1.

335 Pope Benedict XVI, *Declaratio*, February 11, 2013, https://w2.vatican.va/content/benedict-xvi/en/speeches/2013/february/documents/hf_ben-xvi_spe_20130211_declaratio.html.

336 Gerard O'Connell, "Cardinal Arinze praises Pope's courageous decision to resign," Vatican Insider, February 23, 2013, http://www.lastampa.it/2013/02/23/vaticaninsider/eng/news/cardinal-arinze-praises-popes-courageous-decision-to-resign-pgaYNZDHVRAeY9uX45Yz6L/pagina.html.

337 Peter Seewald, *Benedict XVI: Last Testament in His Own Words* (New York: Bloomsbury, 2016), xvii.

338   Brennan Pursell, *Benedict of Bavaria: An Intimate Portrait of the Pope and His Homeland* (New York: Circle Press, 2008), 13.

339   George Weigel, *God's Choice: Benedict XVI and the Future of the Catholic Church* (New York: Harper, 2005), 166.

340   Scott Hahn, "Benedict Will Still Be There for Us," *National Catholic Register*, February 14, 2013, http://www.ncregister.com/daily-news/benedict-will-still-be-there-for-us#ixzz2KzQiOwVn .

341   Joseph Ratzinger, *Faith and the Future* (San Francisco: Ignatius Press, 2009), 116.

342   See Russell Shaw, "Pope Benedict's powerful influence on the Church," OSV Newsweekly, February 13, 2003, https://www.osv.com/OSVNewsweekly/ByIssue/Article/TabId/735/ArtMID/13636/ArticleID/7870/Pope-Benedicts-powerful-influence-on-the-Church.aspx.

343   Weigel, *God's Choice*, 104.

344   Ibid., 119.

345   See Pursell, *Benedict of Bavaria*, 139.

346   Ibid., 140.

347   Ibid., 139–140.

348   Peter Seewald, *Benedict XVI: Light of the World* (San Francisco: Ignatius Press, 2010), 3.

349   Viktoria Somogyi, "George Weigel on 'Deus Caritas Est': Attempt to Introduce 'the God with a Human Face,'" Zenit News Agency, December 19, 2006.

350   Pope Benedict XVI's Address to Pontifical Council "Cor Unum," reported in "Encyclical Aims to Recover Meaning of 'Love,'" *Zenit News Agency*, January 23, 2006.

351   Summary of *Deus Caritas Est*, *L'Osservatore Romano* (Weekly Edition in English), April 26, 2006, https://www.ewtn.com/library/Doctrine/sumdeuscarit.htm.

352   See Pope Benedict XVI, *Deus Caritas Est* ("God is Love"), December 25, 2005, http://w2.vatican.va/content/benedict-xvi/en/encyclicals/documents/hf_ben-xvi_enc_20051225_deus-caritas-est.html, 2. [Hereafter *DCE*].

353   *DCE*, 2.

354 Ibid., 3.

355 Ibid.

356 Ibid., 4.

357 See Ibid.

358 Ibid.

359 Ibid.

360 See *Catechism*, 362.

361 *Gaudium et Spes*, 14.

362 See *DCE*, 5.

363 Ibid.

364 See Ibid.

365 Ibid., 8.

366 Ibid., 7.

367 Ibid.

368 Karol Wojtyła, *Love and Responsibility* (San Francisco: Ignatius Press, 1993), 41.

369 *DCE*, 11.

370 Ibid., 12, emphasis added.

371 Summary of *Deus Caritas Est* in *L'Osservatore Romano*.

372 *DCE*, 14.

373 Ibid., 17.

374 Ibid., 18.

375 Ibid.

376 Ibid.

377 Ibid., 19.

378 Ibid., 25.

379 Ibid., 28.

380 Ibid., 35.

381 Ibid., 39.

382   Simcha Fisher, "Papamoon!" *National Catholic Register*, March 14, 2013, http://www.ncregister.com/blog/simcha-fisher/papamoon#ixzz2Nk4OM64n.

383   Austen Ivereigh, "Pope Francis takes fresh approach to papacy," *OSV Newsweekly*, March 20, 2013, https://www.osv.com/OSVNewsweekly/ByIssue/Article/TabId/735/ArtMID/13636/ArticleID/7879/Pope-Francis-takes-fresh-approach-to-papacy.aspx.

384   Austen Ivereigh, *The Great Reformer: Francis and the Making of a Radical Pope* (New York: Henry Holt and Company, 2014), Kindle edition.

385   Pope Francis, *Evangelii Gaudium* ("The Joy of the Gospel"), November 24, 2013, https://w2.vatican.va/content/francesco/en/apost_exhortations/documents/papa-francesco_esortazione-ap_20131124_evangelii-gaudium.html, 16.

386   Ivereigh, *The Great Reformer*.

387   Paul Vallely, *Pope Francis: The Struggle for the Soul of Catholicism* (New York: Bloomsbury, 2015), Kindle edition.

388   The word "synod" derives from the union of two Greek words, *syn* which means "together," and *odòs* which means "path or journey."

389   A General Assembly of the Synod of Bishops is called "extraordinary" when it is convened to deal with matters "which require a speedy solution" and which demand "immediate attention for the good of the entire Church." See USCCB, http://www.usccb.org/issues-and-action/marriage-and-family/2014-2015-synods-of-bishops-on-the-family.cfm.

390   A copy of this survey can be found at the Vatican website (Pastoral Challenges to the Family in the Context of Evangelization, Preparatory Document), http://www.vatican.va/roman_curia/synod/documents/rc_synod_doc_20131105_iii-assemblea-sinodo-vescovi_en.html

391   Vallely, *Pope Francis: The Struggle for the Soul of Catholicism*.

392   Paul Vallely, *Pope Francis: Untying the Knots* (New York: Bloomsbury, 2015), 334.

393   Ibid.

394   Mary Jo Anderson, "What I Saw at the Synod and What it Means for 2015," *Crisis* magazine, October 23, 2014, https://www.crisismagazine.com/2014/saw-synod-means-2015.

395   George Weigel, "What Really Happened at Synod 2015," *First Things*,

January 2016, https://www.firstthings.com/article/2016/01/what-really-happened-at-synod-2015.

396   Timothy O'Malley, "The Joy of Love: 9 Moments to Savor in *Amoris Laetitia*," *Church Life Journal*, April 8, 2016, https://churchlife.nd.edu/2016/04/08/joyoflove/.

397   Jim Russell, "Pope Francis' 'Time Is Greater Than Space': What Does It Mean?" *Aleteia*, May 24, 2016, https://aleteia.org/2016/05/24/pope-francis-time-is-greater-than-space-what-does-it-mean/.

398   Francis, *Evangelii Gaudium*, 223.

399   Jim Russell, "Pope Francis' 'Time Is Greater Than Space': What Does It Mean?"

400   Pope Francis, *Amoris Laetitia* ("The Joy of Love"), March 19, 2016, https://w2.vatican.va/content/dam/francesco/pdf/apost_exhortations/documents/papa-francesco_esortazione-ap_20160319_amoris-laetitia_en.pdf, 307. [Hereafter *AL*.]

401   Guillaume Goubert and Sébastien Maillard, "INTERVIEW Pope Francis," *La Croix*, May 17, 2016, trans. Stefan Gigacz, https://www.la-croix.com/Religion/Pape/INTERVIEW-Pope-Francis-2016-05-17-1200760633.

402   Dr. John Grabowski, "There's a Lot to Like in *Amoris Laetitia*," *National Catholic Register*, April 7, 2018, http://www.ncregister.com/daily-news/theres-a-lot-to-like-in-amoris-laetitia.

403   Ibid.

404   Ibid.

405   *AL*, 49.

406   Ibid., 1.

407   Ibid.

408   Ibid., 2.

409   Ibid., 3.

410   Ibid., 8.

411   Holy See Press Office, "Summary of the post-Synodal apostolic exhortation *Amoris Laetitia* (The Joy of Love) on love in the family," April 8, 2016, https://press.vatican.va/content/salastampa/en/bollettino/pubblico/2016/04/08/160408b.html.

412   *AL*, 31.

413   Holy See Press Office, "Summary of the post-Synodal apostolic exhortation *Amoris Laetitia* (The Joy of Love) on love in the family."

414   *AL*, 33–34.

415   Ibid., 78.

416   Holy See Press Office, "Summary of the post-Synodal apostolic exhortation *Amoris Laetitia* (The Joy of Love) on love in the family."

417   *AL*, 89.

418   Holy See Press Office, "Summary of the post-Synodal apostolic exhortation *Amoris Laetitia* (The Joy of Love) on love in the family."

419   Ibid.

420   *AL*, 104.

421   Ibid., 106.

422   Ibid., 164.

423   See Holy See Press Office, "Summary of the post-Synodal apostolic
exhortation *Amoris Laetitia* (The Joy of Love) on love in the family."

424   *AL*, 197.

425   Ibid., 199.

426   Ibid., 203.

427   Ibid., 232.

428   Ibid.

429   Ibid., 234.

430   Ibid., 244.

431   Ibid.

432   Ibid., 246.

433   Ibid., 251.

434   Vallely, *Pope Francis: The Struggle for the Soul of Catholicism*.

435   *AL*, 260.

436   Ibid.

437   Ibid., 261.

438   Ibid., 283.

439   José Granados, Stephen Kampowski and Juan José Pérez-Soba, *Accompanying, Discerning, Integrating: A Handbook for the Pastoral Care of the Family According to Amoris Laetitia*, trans. Michael J. Miller (Steubenville, Ohio: Emmaus Road, 2017), Kindle edition.

440   *AL*, 291.

441   Pope Francis references the final report of the 2014 Extraordinary Synod of Bishops more than fifty times and the 2015 Ordinary Synod of Bishops more than eighty times.

442   See *AL*, 3.

443   Granados, Kampowski and Pérez-Soba, *Accompanying, Discerning, Integrating*.

444   *AL*, 293.

445   Ibid., 298.

446   Ibid., 299.

447   Holy See Press Office, "Summary of the post-Synodal apostolic exhortation *Amoris Laetitia* (The Joy of Love) on love in the family."

448   *AL*, 294.

449   Granados, Kampowski and Pérez-Soba, *Accompanying, Discerning, Integrating*.

450   Ibid.

451   See Ibid.

452   Ibid. (Quoting *AL*, 211, 39, 124)

453   Ibid.

454   *AL*, 243.

455   Ibid., 325.

456   O'Malley, "The Joy of Love: 9 Moments to Savor in Amoris Laetitia."